Abhay Khemka is the founder of Khemka Investments and Properties (property advisory services) based in Gurgaon. He has been in business since 1980 and has spent two decades in exports and fifteen years in the real estate industry. His experience tells him that to succeed in business, one has to be spiritual and take decisions from the core and not from the mind. *Punter Learns to Rock* is not only a book but an experience for individuals who believe in seeking.

PUNTER LEARNS TO ROCK

ABHAY KHEMKA

PARTRIDGE

To order additional copies of this book, contact
Partridge India
000 800 10062 62
orders.india@partridgepublishing.com

www.partridgepublishing.com/india

There is no real reason to write this book.

I am not a preacher, nor do I believe that I alone hold all the knowledge. Everybody is borne with subconscious knowledge; perhaps one needs a reminder of what you may have forgotten. This is my understanding of my spirituality.

Every soul is complete and knows everything, but sometimes with a knock on the door awareness comes. You come out of your slumber, awareness brings the required shift in your consciousness and from there change starts taking place. This awareness that brings about change is what I call 'Chetna', which brings awakening.

I was always considered a flamboyant boy in high school and college. I graduated from St. Xavier's College, Bombay. Although I took up math honours, I attended mostly arts classes and visited the canteen more regularly, which resulted in invitations to dance parties, which I was very fond of.

A minimum of four hours of daily dancing and copying John Travolta in *Saturday Night Fever* in front of a full-sized mirror became my daily routine. My hairstyle and walk had become no less than that of Travolta. Once I even danced on various tables joined together at the college canteen.

I spent most of free the time playing cricket since I was in the college team, and I truly loved flaunting my college cap. It was in my second year of college that I took up drinking. I would often go to Delhi for my business, which was a garment export house that I started in 1980.

My first trip abroad was on the day I received my passport. I remember visiting London with my friend, and the immigration officer at Heathrow kept flipping through the pages of my passport, which was totally empty and had no visas stamped on it from any country. We had planned to see Europe, and we did it in the end, without any visa, without any hassle. Anyway, drinking on that trip was a breath of fresh air; we were out of our minds all the time.

Well, the export business did not take off even after I had made six or seven trips to Austria. By this time, every person in my family had written me off. I knew this was going to be my last trip, and I had to go back home with a buyer.

I was at McDonald's by the end of my last trip, under pressure to perform, and that was when I met a gentleman from Pakistan; he was a newspaper seller. He had been there since 1960 and was a distributor for all Asian newspapers.

Since he owned a house and a car, I thought he could be my man, not because of his capabilities, but because of his possessions. I thought I could have an office at his house and a chauffeur-driven car for making sales calls. The idea worked; he agreed to be my importer. Soon I began shipping goods to him, followed by flying to the city and selling them to wholesalers like myself, till I found an Indian buyer.

In 1984, I lost all my money to an Italian firm, which took my goods on L/C but later refused to make payments because DHL lost my documents in transit, and the L/C couldn't get encashed. I was bankrupt and had to start from negative, with bank loans on my head, but then to my rescue came an Indian who had settled in Greece. He gave me cash in advance and bought like crazy from us, as though he was in a hurry to pay off my losses.

In two years, I covered all my losses and even paid the bank. The same Indian Austrian buyer introduced me to somebody in Germany, an Indian also who duped me for whatever I shipped to him; but one day, someone who used to buy from him contacted us and started buying from us directly. This buyer, a German, continued to do business with us for fifteen years, till the gentleman grew old.

So until 1998, everything went well. So until 1998, everything went well. Sipping wine in a five star and travelling to Europe six to eight times a year, life was good and kicking. I had made good amount of money too.

In 1998 came a policy change by the government, in which a retailer abroad could open an office in India, and that was when garment exports died a natural death, I believe.

I received a cassette of Swami Parthasarathy in 1998, from somewhere, and the first line of that cassette was 'Brain is like a child and you got to control it'. I stood up; it was something I had never thought of. Never had I ever believed that there is a god or that spirituality ever existed on this planet.

His words hit me hard. I planned a trip to see him in his Pune ashram, but he was in the United States, so we couldn't meet him. I forgot about it later. My wife, Preeti, heard somewhere about a Satguru and a movement called Art of Living, but I had reservations about these Babas.

One day in 1999, she made a plan with an army major who had taken the Art of Living course, who landed at my house one evening to explain what it is all about. His explanation was pretty pathetic, and the only thing he taught me was that a deep breath in *Ujjai* can be very long.

Just for yoga classes, I reluctantly said yes. Yoga had always impressed me, and I was quite regular with my asanas, but this type of breathing I had never encountered. On the first three days, I kept nagging at my wife that all this was rubbish, until for the first time I did Sudarshan Kriya, a breathing technique designed by Guruji.

I was stunned and went into silence for the remaining three days. It was an experience that was out of this world. My claims about yoga that I had been doing for the last twelve years looked so shallow. We did the basic course on 9 December and went on for the advanced course in Rishikesh in March 1999, where I also met Guruji and asked him to be my Guru and take me as his disciple as well.

He pulled my ears and tapped me on my head. I was thrilled. I guess I had been looking for a Guru for over two years and didn't know how to find one. The joy I felt was fulfilling. Also, by now the Guru in me had not totally grown, and doubts were engulfing me with various questions. I then started listening to a cassette of Guruji's talks and read the books of knowledge available in Art of Living.

My daily routine involved listening to one cassette every day. Besides, my practices, meditation, and silence were still at the infancy stage but had begun to work slowly and gradually. With more and more listening to cassettes, I realised I had started giving out knowledge to everyone about everything.

Soon in my office, my brothers had started to shut me out, telling me they had heard enough of Guruji. My friends also started telling me the same. I couldn't help it.

Knowledge doesn't get digested that easily; you become restless when you meet the truth, but all this knowledge, as Guruji explains, as stored knowledge, is like exam knowledge. It's of no use, only good for textbooks. Intellectually, I started having all the answers to every person's arguments and doubts about issues, until I realised that unless knowledge is experienced, it doesn't become your wisdom.

Once wisdom comes, your textual knowledge disappears, there are no arguments left, and for sure you can say this happens. God is also your personal experience; then there is no scope of doubt. It's like someone explains the pain in your leg; you know how and when it comes, but you don't know how it occurs.

For argument's sake, you may argue about the occurrence of the pain but not about the feeling.

This doubt remains, until you have it yourself. Then there is no argument left. You can say it happens, without a doubt. Spirituality is the same. It starts with a doubt because you doubt the positive; you never doubt the negative.

If I were to tell you, 'I hate you', or 'I am angry with you', you never doubt it; but if I say, 'I love you', your reaction would be, 'Do you?', 'Really?', and so on. The fact about doubt is the more doubt you have, the more faith it will generate, so doubt is not a negative thing. In fact, your faith can't be eternal or airtight unless you have doubted to the brim. Faith is always based on the shoulders of doubt.

The mind clings to the negative, and clinging to the negative is a prime property of the mind. Even if someone tells you one million times, 'I love you', and only once he insults you, you tend to keep that insult in a safe deposit and make an FDR of the same. You will forget that 'I love you', but you will always remember that insult.

This is the way our mind is conditioned by the prevailing circumstances of society. Here, I have to make sure that I am not saying that society is teaching us wrong things; this is the conditioning of the mind.

If we reverse this doubt in the negative, things could change dramatically for all of us. If one says he hates you, doubt that. He may be tense; he probably doesn't mean it. We can avoid a lot of formation of pain bodies inside of us; we have a habit of chewing on the negative until we form it into fermented emotion. We are generating only toxins and forming pain bodies inside us, ultimately solidifying and converting into dreaded diseases.

During the basic course, we were told two to three things: stop living in the past, don't be a football of others' opinions, and expectations lessen joy. Live in the present. We were given the question 'Who am I?' Keep talking to yourself and asking yourself, 'Who am I?' 'Who am I?' And if you remember these basic things, you will get reminded of them a hundred times over every day, enough to spring up a change.

The advanced course was simply superb. To top it all, the ashram was in Rishikesh, near the Ganges, surrounded by lush green mountains. Such a spectacular view.

We learned two great processes:

A. Silence for three days, which meant not talking to anybody. Now I feel I didn't understand it at all. I guess with the Guru's presence, whether you understand it or not makes no difference, he makes it all up.

B. Meditation: In Hindu, we have three Shastras— Mantra Shastra, Tantra Shastra, and Yantra Shastra— meaning mantra. As we all know, this word comes from *mantri* (the minister), who gives the mantra (sutra or the chant), Tantra the technique, and Yantra the device. So a lot of techniques were taught to us.

After the advanced course, my faith in the Guru skyrocketed. I distinctly remember singing this one bhajan very often ('Mujhko Zameen Aasman Mil Gaye Guru Kya Mile Bhagwan Mil Gaye') very quickly. Without expecting and knowing, we did Sahaj Samadhi with Guruji's sister Bhanu Didi.

My mother, Devine, as I call her, taught us Samadhi so effortlessly that we started with Samadhi as though we just went and sat in the park. What used to seem like a big task was never thought to be so easily taught. Then, she also gave a Guru mantra. She also explained that reciting the mantra before starting the Samadhi and in between when thoughts were troubling or disturbing will help dissolve them. I couldn't believe it, It just happens that way, no doubt.

It just works beautifully. In meditation, you normally focus on form; but in Samadhi, you focus on the formless.

That's the difference. In reality, the formless rules the form. For example, without fragrance, a flower is nothing. Music from a guitar or any instrument is the same—again the formless rules the forms, like taste in fruits and so on. The growth process is also from form to formless. The seed germinates into a plant, and the plant into a tree. The tree gives flowers, and the flowers give fragrance. The final crescendo is formless. God is also formless, unlike our thinking that it's somebody old with white beard up in the sky. At least mentally, someone or something outside you, invariably a male identity or a mental image, is formed. We see it as a second or third person, forms have names. God is beyond both.

The word *God* has been distorted for so many centuries that it has lost its meaning. People who have never even glimpsed at the sacred and the infinite vastness use it with great conviction as if they know what they are talking about, or they, at least, argue as if they know and are the authority on it.

Being or God can never be understood mentally. Being is eternal; God is that formless energy which is eternal and ever and omnipresent. *Aatama* is the Being, you know only when the mind is still in meditation (*Dhyan*) when your attention is fully and intensely in the moment. Being can be felt, or what can be felt is what you are not. Once you come to know you are not the mind, or the emotion, or the organs, or the body, and so on, you come to know.

Being is your very essence, and it is immediately accessible to you as the feeling of your own presence.

The realisation that I am or I am not this or that, but it is, I guess, a step from the mere word *Being* to the experience of Being.

Gradually, the meaning of simple words which I used to seek answers for started coming to me as realisation.

The meaning of detachment, I only understood in six months. And the beauty is, with effort nothing comes to you. It just springs up in you naturally. Generally, we term detachment as *dislike* or *avoiding*, literary detach. In fact, detachment brings you towards freedom. It's a positive term, meaning attachment with no condition, without being anxious about being attached. When the bondage drops, you are detached. So now there were two more questions: what you call bondage and how one can drop it. Later I realised the chewing in the mind, for anything is bondage, and stopping this chewing is dropping, but how was still the question.

Actually, when Sri Parthasarathy had said that the mind is like a monkey and you've got to control it, it was then that I realised that there is a mind also; till then, I had never thought of the mind as a separate entity. You think you are using the mind. Actually, if we see that the mind is using us, we are the slave of our mind.

The word *Maya* means '**the mind**'. *Maya* is a Greek word which means 'measure'; what can be measured is the mind. Everything about the world can be measured, but the formless can't.

Your world is your mind, and for you, the world doesn't exist if it is beyond the perception of the mind. In the same way, a frog in a well was told that there exists an ocean that is a billion times bigger than the well and infinite. The frog laughed it off. Similarly, when Satgurus tells us there exist infinite potential, peace, bliss, joy, and infinite energy, God, we quietly disagree in our minds because we can't perceive it. That's why it doesn't fit our world which is our mind.

The problems of the mind cannot be solved on the level of the mind. This aspect has to be looked at. This will be the beginning of a new era for you. *As you can't treat the mind with the mind, or the mind can't be treated at the level of the mind, let's look at the mind and its properties.*

The first thing is the mind clings to the negative and resists the positive. The mind oscillates between the past and the future.

The mind loves complications. In simplicity it dies, so it never allows you to be simple.

Not being able to stop thinking is an identification with the mind, and it can fool you for life.

Everybody is suffering from it, so it is accepted as normal, but it's not.

This ancient knowledge, which was available to Rishis in our country, unfortunately, is never taught in schools or colleges.

This constant chattering of the subconscious and identification is the root cause of all our problems, be it mental, emotional, or physical.

The ego loves and thrives on it, so it never allows anything to take place. You go on unconsciously identified with it and create the drama of life, of which the end result can only be pain or misery and allows the mind to use you all the time. The mind makes you a slave and uses you all the time. It can go on for life, with the ego being in charge. It is not that you use your mind in a wrong way; you don't use it at all. It uses you and becomes your boss. You get into the delusion that you are nothing, and the mind and the ego being in charge, you are driven towards insanity.

You start putting labels, judgments, mental positions, constant conflicts, definitions, and arguments. The needs of the ego are endless. It feels vulnerable and threatened all the time unless it is in charge. So it lives in a state of fear and want. The mind is a wonderful instrument. The mind is not dysfunctional. Problems come when you seek yourself as the mind and mistake it for who you are. The egoist mind then takes over your whole life and being.

The mind doesn't live in the present.

In fact, there can never be any moment but the now or the present; nothing ever existed outside the now. Nothing ever happened in the past; everything happened in the now. Nothing will ever happen in the future; it will happen in the now. When the future comes, it will come in the now, or it will be the past of tomorrow.

Therefore, obviously, the past and the future have no reality of their own. The now is only what exists, the eternal moment. The past is only a memory; it's gone. It doesn't exist in the now, so stop living in your past. The future is just a projection of your mind based on your past. The future is mind generated and can only bring anxiety, anxiousness, fear or give a false sense of security. Our identification with our mind is the cause of all miseries. This egoistic identification with the mind is making us a hero of our own movie. If you are aware of this fact alone that 'I am not the mind' and 'the mind is playing games with me and showing me a different picture', you come out of this drama and start looking at the mind.

This constant chattering of the subconscious and identification is the root cause of all our problems, be it mental, emotional, or physical.

The ego loves and thrives on it, so it never allows anything to take place. You go on unconsciously identified with it and create the drama of life, of which the end result can only be pain or misery and allows the mind to use you all the time. The mind makes you a slave and uses you all the time. It can go on for life, with the ego being incharge.

It is not that you use your mind in a wrong way; you don't use it at all. It uses you and becomes your boss. You get into the delusion that you are nothing, and the mind and the ego being incharge, you are driven towards insanity.

So many thousands of thoughts come out from us. They simply come and go, like waves in the ocean. Let's do one simple exercise: sit for half an hour and watch all thoughts come and go; you would come to know a lot about your thoughts.

A problem comes when unconsciously we pick one thought from the past or future and then start chewing on it and get into extrapolation.

The best way to get depressed is to sit and start thinking, 'What will happen to me?' I can guarantee you that within a couple of hours, you will get depressed. You get into your small mind, and hence, you are missing the bigger picture, the real picture, because with a small mind, you are in your own movie, which is no good. The moment this Chetna arises, you start watching the games your mind tries to play with you. There is a shift in your consciousness, and this is priceless. At least this has helped me endlessly. We'll take a more detailed view of this aspect later.

See, we have set ideas, concepts, likes, and dislikes about ourselves; and this very thing makes us unhappy. You should try to come out of these strong conceptions and ideas about yourself, which are so deep down to every cell of your being and keep throwing you off balance.

Don't have strong concepts too. Instead of having 'concepts' like I don't like this or that, have 'preferences', like I would prefer tea without sugar; but if it has sugar, there is no need to get upset and boil inside. If you have strong notions about it, you are bothered by it and then move away from being natural.

Another example is what will people and society think. I have my prestige and position in society; I am this or that. If such identifications become very intense, you get caught in them all the time. The ego fuels them. By the way, who has the time to keep a record of you all the time? You can peacefully follow the norms of society by not being chaotic or rebellious, but don't get swallowed by this identity crisis.

You are also unhappy about your bondages (people, relationships, society, situations, circumstances, your own body). Understand that everything is changing. This universe is very dynamic; it's not static. It's not dead, nor does it stop in one place. Only change is permanent. Everything—being, situation, time, your blood, cells, bone marrows—everything. What doesn't change is the present! *Nothing is permanent.* If a patient dies, then a doctor also dies. So if the good dies, the bad also dies. The disciple dies, so does the guru.

You take events as happenings; don't get entangled with them. Many a time a big problem or a hurdle comes, but later it appears to be a joke, or as if it was just simple. I simply got stuck in it and wasted my peace of mind, time, and effort.

Everything is temporary! Look at life as a soap opera. Don't take life as a serious subject. Look at it as it is happening.

Don't become it. Don't base yourself on change and get sucked into it. What needs to be looked at is *what am I getting spent in.*

But there is something which is not changing; there is something in you which is non changing. Change is always seen with reference; you can only see change when something is not changing. That's why you notice the change. Sometimes you look around and say, 'Oh, these kids have grown up so much', or 'This place has become small', because you have not changed inside. Your being doesn't change. Your conscience doesn't change.

The mind works on the theory of polar opposites.

Whatever comes into the mind will have polarity, the opposite poles, like the pendulum of a watch. The swing towards the right is gaining momentum to go to the left and vice versa. The sun is rising, reaching its peak. It's not its permanent position; it is just gaining momentum to set.

Notice that if a tightrope walker bends to the right, he bends towards the left as well to maintain balance, to be in the centre. In the centre, the mind ceases to exist.

Buddha says you should always take the middle path, because any deviation, whether in the positive or negative direction, will have an effect in that direction.

Deviation means you are in the mind, which means you carry a reason in your mind. **To be happy, you don't need a reason; but to be unhappy, there is always a reason.** You need a reason to be unhappy.

If you are in the centre, you are in harmony and you are happy. You are with your axis. In the centre is the axis. Any reason is deviation from it and makes you unhappy. See, deviation has taken place. Now you are no longer with an axis. We see the reason and start to solve that reason with the mind and see it as deviation from the axis. Don't get into right and wrong. This awareness is very important.

With this way of looking at things in which deviation has taken place, you can bring yourself back to the axis; otherwise, you easily get caught up. If you swing to the other pole, which is a natural law, then harmony is also your nature. No effort is required; with effort, you create the swing of polarity. Deviations away from being with your natural self, you become somebody, and that's a problem.

In the advanced course, three days of silence was required for observation. Up to that time, I had no clue that a simple technique for observing silence could generate so much energy in oneself.

Anyway, my best friend was taking the course with me, and we would meet every day during the course and acknowledge each other by nodding. After two days, I went to their hotel near the ashram and sat with them all.

Three of us played dumb charades, which involves an action without a word spoken, until my friend started yelling, 'I want to speak'. He was yelling, 'Ha-ha ho-ho'.

What was noticeable was the power behind his yelling. Although that was the end of observing silence, in a way, it was the beginning of silence. One fact was well established: that silence definitely gives a lot of energy, but beyond this was still unknown to me. In fact, there is nothing beyond silence; everything springs up from silence and goes back to silence. If you see at the helm of every emotion, there is silence—silence of the subconscious, ***the chattering mind!***

What happens when you get angry or mad at someone, and after a while, a total silence? You cry your heart out, then silence! After a lot of laughter, also there is silence.

So you can even say that the peak of every emotion is also silence, isn't it? Everything in this universe springs up in silence and goes back to silence.

It was only later that I discovered that keeping quiet and not talking to anyone was not the silence to be observed; it is the silence of the subconscious, the chattering mind.

In fact, thinking about something for long periods never gets you answers because the mind will complicate matters. It's only in silence that you find answers. If you observe this and start practicing, say, in a discussion when things are complicated and answers are difficult to find, you should give yourself a break and observe a little bit of silence. See how your thinking will change, a new dimension will be found.

Chattering is of the mind, of the subconscious, not of the intellect.

Science comes out of spirituality, not the other way around. Science keeps changing because you don't know everything. At a certain point, how much humans know is what is science for them. What can be proved can be disproved; truth is beyond this. You can't change the truth, and if you can, then you are not talking about truth. It must be your science only, from your mind. If the truth was science, I am sure our gods would have been made and destroyed in our laboratory test tubes. The Lord is beyond science. That's why we never get him. It's beyond proof and beyond time; that's all.

Science is knowing of the little mind; that's why it's not full, or complete and is ever changing. Antibiotics were designed, and then the same were later considered harmful. Same with pesticides—good and then later harmful. ***Truth is truth,*** so to go on an imaginary axis all the time in regard to God is not necessary; it softens your faith and allows doubt to enter and destroy even that little faith you develop.

Remember, doubt is always sitting on the shoulders of faith; truth is not the basis to extrapolate God. It is not your drama or some sort of belief. Infact, there is nothing called belief; belief means doubt exists. Otherwise, if you know it and if it's true, then where is the question of belief? To me, lack of knowledge is belief. When you believe in something, that means you doubt it that much. It's directly proportional to each other. So with truth, there is no belief.

People often say, 'I believe in God'; these are the people who doubt God that much or even more because if you base it on some basis or projection of your mind rather than knowing, you are bound to go astray; it will crumble. Wisdom is not believing in it; it's knowing, after which you don't even require knowing. It drops. It's there; you don't have to remember it each time. Belief is an intellectual thing, a concept of the mind. Faith is not a concept, and you don't have it as a condition or a precondition.

If trust happens between you and the master, then Satsang is possible and faith happens. It's just a situation, not a condition.

Between a child and a mother, there is no existence of belief; they don't believe each other, or they don't doubt each other. They have airtight faith; nothing can seep into it. You know the sun will rise tomorrow, and you know it will; you don't believe or doubt it. With the truth you know, that's it.

Truth is always beyond test.

If you are taking a position in your mind, like a preconceived notion, something like having gone to Vaishno Devi, someone says, 'Let's go climbing or walking up to the temple'. Your reaction is, 'I don't believe in the Goddess that much to take that much pain'. See, both things are taking a position in the mind; climbing up has nothing to do with God. Giving yourself trouble is what God is not looking for. It's a projection of the mind. If climbing could get you God, then everybody will get God. It has nothing to do with God; it's your ego's satisfaction—that's all. Secondly, not wanting to go and negating the belief, again, is the mind's chattering and nothing else. You are going to meet the Goddess, simple. How you reach her has no bearing on her, does it? Mind games make you lose your focus on being with the Goddess.

Keep things simple, rather than getting them into the mind. That's why for me, there is no difference between an Atheist and a Theist; both believe, both doubt, both are in the mind.

Let's not have very stringent rules that you become a slave to it. Rules should be like references or a guide, not a ruler. When rules are becoming your ruler, remember, it's only the ego's drive that is driving you towards insanity. See, Lord Krishna, his crown is a peacock feather. As a ruler and a king, he is so light in the head, like a feather, carrying no weight whatsoever.

Look at it from a mathematical point of view; a ruler (scale) measures all other things but never itself.

Beware of them; never measure yourself— lest you become an egoistic mind.

When you see someone doing something wrong, not as per your set of rules or notions, you tend to go mad and angry. Right and wrong are relative things; what is right for you may be wrong for others and vice versa.

Your action is your state of the mind, and improving your action will not change the state of mind. You need to change the state of your mind, and then the action will change automatically. 'To be with the wrong is also wrong'—a person who is corrupt and a person who is not corrupt but sees that the other person is corrupt are both caught up in the mind.

If you are against something, you have no freedom, and you are equally caught up. What is the difference? You are unnecessarily carrying his filth on your shoulders. Just look at it. That's all. 'Awareness' creates answers.

The mind needs intoxication and wants to get attached easily through five Indriyas (touch, taste, smell, sight, hearing) and lust and greed. In attachment of these, the energy flows outwards and saps you.

When you go inwards, you gain energy, and when you are in the world (going outwards through the mind), you lose energy.

Both a terrorist and a priest are intoxicated—the terrorist for his love for his land and the priest for his religion, knowledge, and a set of rules. Both are in fixation and bondage. The intoxication, stuck at a point in the mind, has no difference. The mind exists. It's not dropped. Life energies are not flowing in them. With the fixation of the mind, Life energies stop flowing and creates blockages in you.

What is suicide? It's getting stuck at one point and thought in the mind. If you are pushed ahead, you become all right. Don't get stuck; *bondage with the good is as good as bondage with the bad* because what is good today may become bad tomorrow. The swing of the pendulum will take place, and Life energies will not be stuck in one place. Change will take place.

Let your life energy in your Being flow like a river.

It's definite that the river meets the ocean, its ultimate destiny. Imagine, if the river starts to use its brain and tries to take shortcuts or get stuck at one point, it will never reach the ocean. In the same way, one should flow like a river and allow the Divine or the infinite to drive you rather than getting driven by our small minds. In the Geeta, the word *surrender* is emphasised. Surrender is not what makes you meek, weak, or smaller; it's not in any way a negative term. Surrender, infact, puts more pressure on the other person to take extra care, like a child by a mother. It's the mother all the time taking care of him.

A child is free of bothering because he has surrendered, until he starts to take a mental position and becomes something. That becoming something starts the *Leela* of his life. What is Leela? Leela is of the mind; what you are is all created by you, no one else, which means one is playing with his mind and creating and destroying himself with his own mind.

Your ego also makes you the hero of your own film. So get out of your own way and surrender. Let the bigger mind take care of you. In any case, what can you really do with this preconditioned ancient mind with past impressions and emotions?

See, if a cockroach is told to leave the body and surrender to God, it will not. Being somebody comes in the way; it will say, 'Why? I am the vice-chancellor of this sewage pipe.' It has no idea that surrender will only make it better than what it is now. What else can it lose from here on? It can only get better, but the mind doesn't allow it. Look at this phenomenon. Surrender doesn't come with effort; it comes with unshakeable faith.

Actually, with effort you get nothing. The mere thinking of making an effort is of the mind. With the mind you can hardly achieve anything. If you see, the intellect and mind has never achieved much in terms of getting to truth, freedom, or peace.

The mind likes distant things.

The mind loses interest when you already have them. Like a shirt in the showroom, when you first see it, you want to possess it, therefore you buy it. However, post purchase it keeps lying in the closet. —'The shirt has lost its appeal in the mind'. The mind loses it's interest once you possess it. That's why a neighbour's wife always attracts you. The grass on the other side is always greener. Osho said that it's very easy to pursue a woman, but it's very difficult to put her aside later on, because she will live in your mind.

Another thing in the advanced course was Meditation. I had this great desire to learn meditation, but I had no clue what Meditation does to you, but it always attracted me. They taught us many techniques, but I liked the Hari Om Meditation best, where they teach you to relax the seven energy centres (the chakras in our body).

The first thing I realised was that meditation really relaxes you, but that's how little I knew of it. After the advanced course, one gets rejuvenated.

Everybody took a dip in the holy Ganga with Guruji; this was simply splendid. I am sure a lot of sins were washed, but this is purely speculation. The water was very cold; I thought I would stay for a minute because I get cramped very easily in cold water. I went in with a strong impression and inhibition but stayed in the water for almost nine to ten minutes. I really felt light and nice.

During the advanced course, you share a room with three to four other people. I was sharing mine with three people from Gujarat. I used to get up late and hence had to use the toilet after everybody else. I used to get irritated the way they used to leave the toilet wet, with water on the seat.

I had recently learned that anger comes with lack of knowledge. This fact, however, I had not experienced yet.

For the first two days, I was upset with my roommates. On the third day, I caught hold of one of them and asked strongly, 'Can't you just lift the seat after you are finished? Why the hell do you guys leave it so dirty?'

He said, 'Sorry, sir, for the last two days we were trying to figure how to we can keep it clean, but we didn't know it was so simple. Next time, we will left the seat and not leave it wet. In any case, this is our first experience with a Western-style toilet.' I was astonished and flabbergasted.

Then I realised anger comes with lack of knowledge. I didn't know that they were not aware, and they were innocent. I was boiling inside over nothing.

If one observes, mostly anger is caused because of not knowing the other persons' position or state of mind. As it happens usually over the phone, I realised many a times such a thing taking place—'Oh, he talked to me so rudely', 'He was dry', 'He put the phone so suddenly', and so on—without knowing the actual position on the other side. Anger comes from lack of knowledge or lack of awareness. Everybody keeps saying, 'Drop your anger'. You can't drop it just like that. You can only sweep dust under the carpet. And one day you will have a volcanic eruption coming out of that stored anger. See, you become aware, and the more aware you become, the more control you have on your anger. You do not have to control it, just by looking at anger, your anger drops. You must have noticed that the moment you become aware—Oh shit, unnecessarily I got angry—it drops.

Another thing of consequence that I realised was that for all other organs in the body except the mind, we have great medical help. We ca get them treated whenever we face a problem with them. For the lungs, heart, liver, stomach, kidney, intestine, and so on, we have enough science to take care of them. But what do we ever do for the mind?

We have never overhauled it for the past so many years; it is with us. That means it must have been full of filth and tired by now. I started thinking about it very seriously and got a little saddened that nobody ever told me that you can take care of your mind also, or at least know how to give it rest sometimes.

It's been working for too many years; you are now aware of this fact. This awareness gradually starts to deepen. It's now a way of life with me rather than a conscious effort.

After the advanced course, one day I was listening to a cassette, *Life beyond Death*, by Guruji. He explained that the strongest and deepest impression in a human being is that of death. The last impression that you carry is what you will start your next life with. It is the deepest impression you carry in your current life. Many times we notice that the last thing you remember before sleep is the first thing that you wake up with.

No wonder a mouse will only become a cat because its strongest impression is the fear of a cat. A cat can only become a dog. In the end, since a lion or tiger has no such fear or impression, the buck stops here.

People are amazed by how a person gets drowned in water, since water has buoyancy—it can only throw things up and not drown anybody. It's our fear of death that we get drowned in.

Look at a corpse, always floating on the surface—how in death you can float and not when you are alive. It's only your fear in the mind which makes you drown. We have also seen children come up. At times, we hear in a dreadful car accident that the parents, unfortunately died, but the infant came out unscratched. It never had any fear in the mind. The infant was one with the whole universe. There was no interference with the event. The event passed through it.

'What you resist, persists.'

After the advanced course, very shortly I did the DSN, privately with one of the teachers from Bombay and Sahaj Samadhi.

Listening to one cassette by Guruji or Osho was still my habit. Every evening, this was the done thing. Every morning I would do my practices; after DSN, it would take me an hour to do yoga, Kriya, and Meditation. In DSN, they teach you Padma Sadhana. It's a combination of all three very strong and potent practices; you could really feel fearless and energetic for the whole day. A half year passed; I also got over the initial boredom of sitting in Meditation. I started enjoying it now, but any spiritual experience or event where you see growth was still eluding me.

I was also hankering for a Guru story or experience of the Guru's grace. I started enjoying Meditations/Samadhi, at least I had started experiencing a mind with no thoughts or very little thoughts.

We all want freedom, but actually speaking freedom from what? We want freedom from our own minds, end of the thoughts, bombardments—that is, freedom from unwanted mind chattering. To be happy, you do not require a reason. If you are happy, that's your nature and surely there has be a reason to be unhappy. If you have a thought or a reason, your happiness goes. God has not created humans that they remain unhappy, how you would never want that your children are unhappy. In the same way, God must be feeling miserable seeing all of us unhappy. The whole creation and every action in this creation are the results of joy and happiness. It's like in every action of ours, we seek out joy, so much so that suicide is committed with the thought of receiving peace and happiness afterwards.

Actually, *your action should be an expression of joy* and not to seek joy out of it. Otherwise it has an expectation of it, and 'expectation lessens joy'. When an action is done, expecting a certain result, you become feverish of the desired result. Let's say you want to go to Bombay and you start off with 'Oh, I am going to Bombay! I am going to Bombay!' This feverishness will kill the joy, or for all you know, you'll land in a mental hospital. You simply start your journey. You may stop on the way, eat, drink, and reach Bombay. You will enjoy. You are in the moment, but if you are feverish, you will miss the moment, miss the joy.

Happiness is an expression of joy, a state where you feel something inside you has expanded, giving a feeling of fulfilment, for which you do not have to make tall plans. Usually, we postpone it for the future, like 'I will be happy when this or that thing will happen', 'When I will pass my twelfth standard with distinction', 'When I will get a job', 'When I get married to my soulmate'. What soul mate when you have not even met your own soul or self?

If you notice, the only thing that you have done is first have a demand and then wait anxiously for that to happen to your satisfaction. Usually, it never does; it does not happen the way you perceive it. You become miserable, start to curse yourself or your luck, become extremely religious, and so on. What you have to understand is that you were postponing your happiness. The mind likes distant things; be happy right now and forever. The word *Vishya* means matter or reason, but you see, the first four letters form 'vish' (poison). If there is a reason, there is poison in the first place. Don't have attachments of desired results in your mind; accept it the way it is, which is acceptance of the fact. That is being spiritually mature.

Life is to grow, to grow spiritually and not physically. Growing physically will automatically happen. Maturity is not meant for a chosen few; it's meant for everyone, because humans are designed to grow spiritually, emotionally, and physically.

An animal is mature because it has no complexes. Dogs don't have to go to doctors for counselling, or they don't visit plastic surgeons.

Animals have one line of activity; a mature animal never deviates or breaks the laws of nature. Adulthood in humans can't be associated with maturity. Intellect is not maturity.

Infact, intellect alone will bring wickedness in you. As a child, we develop desires, likes, and dislikes. In the Geeta, it's mentioned that our whole life we spend in likes and dislikes; likes will push you towards desires to acquire and possess, in which you feel happy and secure. Dislike is just the opposite in which you feel unhappy and insecure. Many of these likes and dislikes, including some dislikes which give you the feeling of unfulfillment, remain with you as you grow. Some of them mutilate, injure, hurt, and bleed inside us and destroy our personality.

Acceptance with objectivity is maturity.

When you have a situation and are involved, then you do not face facts; you face situations projected by your mind. To manage without getting swayed is maturity. We are quite objective when it comes to someone else. When someone else is involved, then we are all great counsellors. Suppose your friend's wife dies, you go to him and console, saying, 'Death is a fact of life, everyone has to face it', and so on. Then you exactly know what is right and what is wrong. You are also very ethical, as far as the behavior of other people are concerned. You should not be hurt, not insulted, not hated. Nobody should be angry with you. People should be friendly with you and not jealous. People should be compassionate and sympathetic.

And even God should always favor you, when others are involved. You are quite objective.

Let's say when you were a child and had a desire for a toy car, for which you were feverish, and also had fear of losing it. How come when your child comes to you for that toy car, it doesn't bother you? You are no longer feverish or have any fear of losing it because now you have outgrown it and are mature about it, but you are now stuck with your Honda or Mercedes.

Most people are stuck as a ten-year-old child. Before, they talked about how their father is better than yours; now they talk about how their countries are better than yours, their city is greater than yours, their religion is better, and so on. They have not grown, but if you can be mature about the toy car, then you can be mature about anything else. Acceptance of everything is maturity and looking at things objectively will bring maturity.

Let's also look at desire. Desire is never ending unless dealt with. Swamis or Gurus these days tell you to drop your desire. It will not drop like that. There are certain ways, to make it happen. Just by saying drop it, nothing is going to happen.

'Experience of a desire makes the desired drop.'

Looking at desire can make the desire drop, desire has only one function, to multiply and leaves you empty with a bigger desire. If you see the futility of it, it can drop.

From a toy car and water bottle, one comes to real cars or diamonds, where one has grown from one desire to another, from one stage of unfulfillment to another. Desire is linear, from small to big. That's all. Looking at the futility of it, being aware of this futility, it can drop. Hence, there are only two ways to drop desire, one is the experience of it and another is looking at the futility of it.

Otherwise, there will be feverishness. There will only be reactions in your life. If you do not accept facts and grow emotionally, the reaction will happen. It's mechanical. Everyone has it because unfulfillment is there deep inside, triggering reactions. We feel we have outgrown them, but very often it's not the case. We have only given up our pursuit, so they remain and become the nucleus of our personality.

If you just do the action without looking at the result or being feverish about the result, there will be no regret and there will be no reaction. Then one can grow in totality, and that action also will be the right action.

Immediately after an advanced course, my wife came and told me that Guruji was going to be in Rishikesh on Shivratri. We made the program to go to Rishikesh; we took my mother also since we were taking our car. She is a total Shiv Bhakt. I was totally oblivious to what I was going there for. I had never celebrated Shivratri that way, but Guruji being there was a good-enough incentive for me. Getting in the car and driving all the way was never my cup of tea, so I would always take a driver even if I had to travel a short distance.

We reached in the morning, there were probably two thousand people in that Satsang hall, and Guruji was deep in meditation. Satsang was also picking up, and in between, I was going into Meditation. Suddenly, Preeti shook me. 'Look, Guruji is dancing.' I opened my eyes and saw something.

Boy! I was wonder struck, Guruji was dancing like Shiv's Natraj form. I can bet even the original John Travolta or any human can't dance in that way. It was out of this world. Everybody was in a trance and clapping out of daze. I guess I was bowled out without a clue. It was simply divine! You got to be out of your mind to dance like that. Infact, it was very evident that only the dance remained; there was no dancer. I can't explain this; no words can. That's why they say words have limitations. Later, people informed us that Guruji was in meditation for almost two days prior to this. After this, I guess Guruji became the true love of my life.

A month later, we came to know that sessions of Ashtavakra Gita were held at Westend, New Delhi every Sunday, and it would take about three months to finish. This required a group of a minimum of ten people to take part in, luckily, we fitted into it. Never before in my life had I heard the name Ashtavakra Gita. Gita, for me, was always Krishna Geeta of Mahabharata. We started going there and listening to the tapes of Guruji about this Gita that was new to me.

Previously, I had been to a Geeta recital with my mom. They used to call it Bhagwat Bachana, but I always noticed one thing, that these women would never talk about any knowledge afterwards. The only discussions were about the Baalpan (child age) of Krishna, but never about any Gyan (knowledge) Krishna imparted to Arjuna, not even a word.

They would instead discussions trivial matters like the cost of the event and the clothing of the PanditJi. The decoration and the Prasad, everything else was discussed except the knowledge. It was more of a status symbol to host such an event. I even asked my mom this question and very candidly she agreed to what I was saying.

We finished the Ashtavakra Gita in three months, but if I may be allowed here to explain the difference between the two Gitas, I think one word for each can explain the difference. Krishna Gita talks about *Surrender*, while Ashtavakra talks about *Saakshi*, the witnessing consciousness (to witness).

Let's not get into Gita, lest this will be a never-ending book, but what was noticed by me was that Krishna Gita is like poetry. People have made their own interpretations suiting themselves, like what has to happen will happen, you surrender to me, and so on. Now, this in a way drove the entire Hindu community to the non karma theory, but one can't do such tricks with Ashtavakra' s words. They are speaking the truth directly, without mincing words.

One confusion was there, definitely, on my mind: now which one to follow, the Surrender or the Witnessing? I guess knowledge and understanding also manifests in you with time. But one thing about knowledge is very true: it springs up and stands as Sakshi (witness) when you require it. It always does come and stand as Sakshi on all occasions. We ignore it that is a separate story. More often than not, it happened to me later.

With my life experiences, as we go along, I would try and explain this aspect, but whatever I am writing regarding truth is my own realisation and understanding of it. It may still be half-truth because I am not an authority on the subject.

Thankfully, a few months later, we kept the Ashtavakra Gita at our house, but this time around, we discussed the knowledge after each cassette and tried to understand what was said. Of course, I would be the one doing most of the explaining to the rest of the group as it reinstated in me that way, and a better understanding of things had started to take place.

We also listened to Patanjali Yoga Sutra. Yoga doesn't mean a set of exercises only; Yoga is what gives you total harmony of body, mind, and soul. Patanjali was a great sage. He was the master of knowing how the mind functions. Patanjali means when you join both hands together and you form a cup between your palms, it means Anjali, and *Patan* means dropping of desires (Patanjali). Before desires arise, you simply drop them.

Patanjali explains that the mind moves in five modes:

Proof (Pramana): It wants proof all the time. It has three subsets: (a) what is written, generally the mind accepts it; that is what is written in Vedas, Shastras, law books, and so on. (b) The mind accepts that when a lot of people are doing something, we also say not everybody is a fool. (c) Seeing is believing.

Wrong knowledge: 'Why did she say this on the phone?' 'She meant this or that.' 'People hate me.' 'I am ugly.' You interpret things wrongly and away from the truth, your own negative projection of even simple things.

Fantasy: You fantasise, making castles in the air about the future, a thing, or a person.

Smriti: Memory of the past; keep thinking about past events.

Sleep: When the top 4 are not there, you sleep; and when the top 5 are not there, you are in meditation. What can actually trouble you with four things:(1) sex, (2) mind, (3), desires, and (4) fear? And the mind and the ego always want to complicate everything.

What I liked the most about Patanjali is that he says of these five modifications of the mind, either this totality of the mind can lead you into deep anguish or in dukkha (misery), or if you rightly use this mind and its functioning, it can lead you to non misery.

The word *non misery* is very important. Patanjali doesn't say it leads you to Ananda or bliss. He says it because bliss doesn't come from the mind; bliss or being happy is your nature.

It doesn't come from the mind, but when the mind ceases, or once you are in the state of non misery, the inner bliss starts to flow. But that doesn't come from the mind; it comes from your inner being. It's like you open the windows and the rays of the sun enter. By opening the windows, you are not creating sun; the sun was already there. Your window can be your hindrance; the sun rays are outside waiting to enter. Patanjali says, 'Yoga is cessation of the mind'.

When the mind ceases, you are established in your witnessing self. In other states except this, there are identifications, and all identifications constitute the Sansaar, the world in misery. If you have transcended the identifications, you are liberated, and that world is here and now, right now!

The world of bliss, he says, becomes a witness of the mind, and you have entered it. But if you have identified with the mind, then you have missed it. This is the basic definition of yoga. Volumes are written on Patanjali. I am just sharing tiny portions of his sayings which I like very much. With the passage of time, the importance of breath has become more and more established in me. Let's have a look at the following: What was the first act we did coming to this world? We took in a breath and then cried. And on our last act, we breathe out and make others cry.

This is a popular example of Sri Sri. Our one complete breath means breathing in, sustaining, and breathing out. They say Brahma, Vishnu, and Mahesh are there in one breath. Brahma is the creator. When we breathe, we rejuvenate and create *prana*, the vital life energy. Keeping it in, that is. maintains, is the Vishnu, and breathing out, Mahesh the destroyer. We take out toxins when we breathe out, so one should be aware of his breath.

We are not even breathing properly. We only generally utilize 14 percent of our lung capacity. Breath is the link between the body and the remaining layers of our consciousness. *Prana* means the point at which your breath meets your consciousness, which generates *Prana*, the vital life force energy. Our emotions are linked to our breath; every emotion has a particular breathing pattern. When we are sad, our breathing pattern is different. When we are angry, the pattern is different. When you are anxious, your pattern is different, and so on. When you are at peace, your breath is in harmony.

This means that if you can control your breathing pattern, keep breath harmonized, you can also control your emotions.

That also means that emotions are just deviations of breath, **when they come back** to their axis, and you become happy and at peace. Then you can say that emotions have no value. They are just a deviation from harmonized axis, and that's why Buddha said, 'You have to do nothing but just be with your breath, that's all'.

In the basic and advanced course, we learned that push buttons will be pressed by Guruji constantly. Push buttons mean testing whether you get irritated and disturbed or not. Well, this was my interpretation of the push button. To the extent I never knew, as you progress, the push buttons are pressed even harder to test your knowledge and endurance. Heavenly people or folks are not gullible or naive that you can fudge anything with them, they will put it to test.

Push buttons, as far as my business was concerned, got pressed immediately after my basic course. Now, I was almost halfway through, and I had already done three different businesses and shut them.

After twenty years in garments exports, which died its natural death in 1998, I was on a lookout for a new line of activity. Life in general was going on but not somewhat smoothly for me. I transferred my office from Panchsheel to the GK enclave. I had bought from a friend the back portion of a basement, and my friend occupied the front. He was running a share brokerage firm; we were in the same social club and good friends.

The only issue was that water would seep in during monsoon. Despite knowing this fact, I still bought the office. **Eventually because of the same problem, I had to sell and go elsewhere later.**

Since I did not have much work, I would go to his office and gradually got interested in the share market. We were friends from before, but now being together for most of the day, we became much closer.

Soon, another gentleman joined the company, who used to have inside information regarding the share market. On the basis of which, he was doing very well and making a lot of money. He was picking up stocks in large quantities like there was no tomorrow.

I had also made good money by now. For few months I kept telling my friend I couldn't cope up and would quit, but just seeing how the other gentleman was performing, I was sticking on. Finally I decided to quit and asked for my cheque from them. About 30 percent of the cheque I had taken, but the rest of the payment was to come within ten days. Usually, I would do small quantities, and this fellow would buy as if there was no tomorrow, somehow to show that even I could do such quantities. I ordered some large quantities to be bought in my account, and the next morning, as luck would have it, the market opened with a freeze in the reverse way. With no buyers, sellers freeze and then it kept on falling. In a week's time, it was 60 percent down with me sitting on huge stocks. Never in my life had I done quantities like that. I had completely lost my mind by then.

At home, there was so much unrest and emotional breakdown. I was a total wreck by now. I went into

Abhay Khemka

depression and didn't know what to do—wait or sell the stocks. They were falling each day, like a one-way traffic. Even if I would make up my mind to go and sell, I couldn't say 'sell' in front of the monitor; I would tremble. This time my friend was also insisting that I should sell and I sold eventually, but it was rather late in the day.

I lost a huge sum of money. It was imperative to manage that money overnight. I had some securities with them, which I had not collected from them as payment was to come in ten days, so that was adjusted for balance. I had no plan, and no cash was there.

Although my money was invested in property, there was no cash flow. I sold my new car and got some money, still some balance was left. It was a huge hit for me since I didn't possess that kind of liquidity. Also, in the last four years, I was eating out of my capital. A lot of money also sank in giving loans to people who never returned even a cent. I must have helped twenty known jokers to construct their homes at various places for some reason as I was acting as Mother India. I had this habit of becoming a messiah for everyone.

Now, I needed a messiah desperately, but there was none. I was more bothered by the fact that I had no right to put my children's future in jeopardy because of the mindless things that I had done. All knowledge and everything was down the drain. I was going down every minute and would just cry every half hour.

My brother came over from Bombay. He said that one of his business associates' was at the Park Hotel in

Goa, who had previously been in the UK. He was basically from Goa and was the son of an ex-chief of the army. I went to see him. He made me feel like he was the messiah I had been searching for and Goa was the land of opportunities.

So I planned a trip to Goa, with the thought of Prāyaścitta deep in me. Since I didn't know what to do next, I accepted that whatever came naturally to me would be the right thing for me.

I was thrown off balance by this event. A lot of it was my belief that I was under the umbrella of my guru, so whatever happened, at least I would not perish; and if I perished, then I couldn't do anything against the divine will. That's why they say there's no harm in tagging along God. He's with you all the time. If you fall, you will not get fragmented. God as hope will come and stand as Sakshi. Even if you are successful, you will not become egoistic. In this way both good and bad can be taken as divine will. Obviously, destiny has a role to play as well.

Guruji says, 'If you are in such a whirlpool of emotions, then take a full dip. Let it touch the bottom. Don't resist. Then only you can come up. Otherwise, in the middle you remain caught up in the whirlpool.'

In any case, I was very close to the bottom, if not at the bottom. During a conversation, where probably I was trying to draw emotional support from my friend subconsciously, I got the Sutra when she said, 'You have become a case of self-pity'.

She was in no way giving any support, but she unconsciously gave me the Sutra. Immediately there was a shift in my consciousness, and I distinctly remember I was lying down and talking on the phone, and I got up. Doors got opened. I wasn't a closed circle anymore, and now, I wasn't all that meek and weak. Her mother met me for dinner and said, 'So what if you have fallen? Everybody does. But a man will get up and fight again. The way you get up is what matters and not the fall.' This was a big Sutra for me. 'Every fall is for growth.' Guruji's words started to come to my mind: 'It's the way you get up or rise after the fall that makes you a man'.

If one takes it as the divine's will, then you have nobody to blame, not even yourself, you can't go out and start fighting with stars and planets; then an understanding comes and you accept your fate.

I wasn't caught up in it anymore, but scars were there, still there. Pain was there, but intensity was losing its grip on me. As Osho explained understanding, somebody put up this question for Shri Bhagwan: 'When you ask us to understand something clearly, whom do you address? To understand, the mind has to cease. Therefore, it is not making the mind understand anything. Who should understand then?' He said, 'Yes, the mind has to cease, but it has not ceased yet. The mind has to be worked on.'

An understanding has to be created in the mind. Through this understanding; this mind will die. That understanding is just poison for the mind then. You are the taker, and the poison kills the mind. The mind understands this, but the understanding is a poison for the mind. That's why the mind resists it so much. It tries and tries not to understand, it creates doubts, and it fights. In every way, it protects itself because understanding is a poison. If understanding happens, then the mind has to die. The mind has to understand and not you.

You need not understand, with understanding the mind dies. Understanding also disappears. You are again centred. Understanding is just a persuasion for the mind and not to fight the mind. With this fight you are caught up with, the mind will never leave you. All teachings and meditations are a deep persuasion for the mind.

Ancient Rishis saw this phenomenon; that is, when the mind reaches such understanding, it drops.

They also say that the mind comes out of any shock in twelve days. That's why after death, we have mourning period of twelve days, and on the thirteenth day there is a celebration, and a feast is cooked. It's in the system and is inbuilt to bring you back to the core only if you allow the natural law to take place. But if you get caught up and allow the mind to be in charge of you, then you don't come out of it.

I realised that the mind is the only gainer in this case, and for the mind, this was Christmastime. It loves to chew on the whole thing over and over. I realised that I am not the mind. This Chetna allowed me to take this as a happening and stopped identification and the mind from labelling it any further. Actually, heavenly folks gave me a tough paper this time around, something like if you receive an IIT paper in your eleventh standard.

Here, I was hit with the emotional problem of the lowest to the highest order. On the other hand, I was cleaned up with my money, almost nowhere to run. Fighting back was difficult. Since there was no business running for me at this time for the last few years, I was so fed up with these emotional problems, so much so that very often I would say, 'I will leave and go'.

Also, I decided that Prāyaścitta had to be done, which simply means Prayas (effort) with the Chitta (consciousness). Turn the Chitta around, turn the consciousness upside down.

Since I had seen that the mind was having a good time with me, now it was evident that I not only had two types of problems but also had the third type, the mind, which was taking me down by the minute.

So I decided to tackle them one by one. The first thing was as we talked, your action is your state of mind. *By improving the action, nothing will happen. You have to improve the state of mind.*

This constant chattering of the mind needs to be shut. This identification with the mind needs to be dropped. Then all the stored knowledge starts to come and stand as Sakshi. With sacred knowledge, one thing is for sure: it will test you and then come to your rescue, but the choice of whether to take it or not remains with you. In this depressing state of the mind, I was going into silence more often than not. Well; this was the natural phenomenon of yourself to bring you back.

I was getting cooked in my mind. I started to witness, from a little distance, like a watcher, and see what it does. Thoughts were bombarding me, the same way the US bombarded Iraq.

I realised that the thoughts were coming and going, mostly negative ones, but a few times, subconsciously, I would get caught up with them, and then, I was becoming my mind. That thought and extrapolation would happen with the speed of light. Slowly, by looking at the mind and the games it was playing.

It was my opportunity to put my knowledge to use. Eventually, in a month's time, I got rid of one problem, which was my own mind. I was ready to fightback.

I started to harmonise my breathing pattern, and gradually I noticed that emotions were subsiding and the intensity was becoming less and less. In retrospect, we see that emotions have no value and are just the deviation from our axis. **Then why get caught up with them and be in misery?**

Love is not an emotion. Love is something that you are made up of, meaning when you are with the axis, love is there. If there is any deviation, it vanishes. Love is your nature; the rest of the emotions then are distorted versions of love.

Our Puranas say that rhythmic breathing, if practiced, can set your breath back on its axis and can get you out of constant and compulsive repetitive thought patterns. That's why so much emphasis is put on Pranayama.

Pranayama means the Vayayam, the exercise of the *prana* or the breath (Prana, Vayayam). Why Buddha put so much emphasis on watching one's breath is that the moment you watch your breath, you would notice that thoughts stop. You can practically try this. Watch your breath and see your mind with no thoughts.

If our breath is numbered, then why breathe fast and invite death much faster than it is supposed to come? Just breathe slow and deep. This way, you not only increase your lifespan but also eliminate many diseases and can come to the axis fast.

Everything has a rhythm. The cosmos has a rhythm. Your body/breath has a natural rhythm. When you are with it, you are in harmony, not only with yourself, but also with the cosmos. Then you are one with the whole. Otherwise, you are cut off; you are alone.

The entire Ramayan happens every minute in your body. *Ram* means consciousness, *Sita* means soul. *Laxman* means Chetna, awareness.

When the soul crosses the line of awareness, Ravan, the ego, arrives. In the ego, you have many heads. You are not one; you are divided. And the ego takes the soul away. What and who brings it back?

The Hanuman, or your breath, brings the soul back to the conscious (axis).

Vibhishana, younger brother of Ravan, or the ego, says that giving up the material world (golden Lanka), to be with the consciousness, which is Ram, it's worth it. This Ramayan keeps happening to us all the time.

When we say the mind cannot be treated at the level of the mind, a question only comes out of the mind. All it does is lead to another question—why, what, when, and so on. Then there is no end to this. **We have to go beyond this. When you are not in the mind and with your spirit, then bliss and peace are the natural outcomes.** You don't require any effort to attain them.

The mere making of an effort to attain them makes you enter the mind. When you are in the mind, you completely miss it. *Spirituality is not making any effort.* You have to make no effort to be with your spirit; just be with it. Your being is all that you are looking for. It is at that point at that you stop all the 'whats, whens, and whys'. You are complete and in the moment, which is called eternal, where you don't create any physical time of past and future; you go beyond time.

Up until now, we understand that you are not in your childhood; it has come and gone. You are not in youth; that has also come and gone. You are not an emotion; emotion also has a short life of a few days. It also comes and goes. You are not the mind; you are not any thoughts. It is like waves of the ocean; it comes and goes. You are not the football of others' opinions or even your opinion; that also keeps changing. You are not in possession of anything; that only strengthens the ego.

You are not the body; it perishes, but you are eternal. Even when you surrender; it doesn't come through effort. You are not anger; that's not your permanent state of being. You are not society's norms and rules; they change with time and place. You are not even religion; they are a set of rules a community and not universal.

You are not a life situation; *that is also impermanent.* You are not money; money is also a source of means. Neither are you a machine that accumulates money; you don't take money along with you. You are no event in your life, good or bad; they come and go. You are not a relationship either; it changes.

Now, wonder comes and not a question: who am I? You are wonderstruck. Wonder is wonder; it doesn't lead you to another question. You are out of your mind; you have transcended the mind. Now you are free. Then bliss, peace, love, and joy are the natural outcomes; and that's what your being is. You are just a being, a plain, simple being, without any label or tag attached to it. You are then free.

I took a flight to Goa and had a look at a couple of projects, but we zeroed in on opening a multiplex. We went to find out the tax structure on the tickets and found out that they had some weird 60 percent tax, and at that moment, the project was shelved. I was coming back to Delhi. The next morning, my friend was dropping me at the airport.

We were crossing the Mandovi River when he showed me two vessels/boats from the bridge and reluctantly said, 'If you would like to take over these boats, it's a good business'. Spontaneously I said yes. We crossed the bridge, and he took us to the office of the Director of Tourism of Goa. Upon enquiring, the director said in a month's time, he would be requesting for tender for the said boats. We could apply then. Guruji was visiting Delhi after ten days, and I went to see him. I had never asked any personal questions, but since I was at a crossroads, I thought it would not be a bad idea to ask him. Guruji was staying at Westend at a devotee's house. I stood right in front of him and asked, 'Guruji, there is this proposal in Goa regarding boats. Shall I go ahead?'

He stopped and looked at me, and after a two- to three-second gap, he gave me a nod. In the affirmative, I knew I was running these boats in Goa. Nevertheless, after a few days with my Delsey bag, which contained a few clothes, I landed in Goa on 27 November 2000.

I had informed my friend about my arrival, but there was no sign of him at the airport. He didn't show up. After waiting for two hours, I gave a call to his house to find out his whereabouts. His wife picked up and said that he didn't receive my message and that I should take a cab and come. This was the turning point of my life. I could have easily lived in my property as most people would have.

Since that nod of Guruji, I had so much faith that I was supposed to do this. My first lesson of expectation lessened my joy, which came along with my friend not coming. His home was some sixty kilometres away from the airport. The drive in the cab took me one and a half hours, but it was breathtaking. Greenery all along had a major pull of energy, nature at its best.

I had initially thought I could stay with him for a few days, but upon reaching his place, I realized I had to check in at a hotel right away. It was also made clear by him that in no certain terms would I check in at a hotel near his house. That also made sense; I have never stayed with my relatives in my life.

I also preferred it that way; tender was to be opened in four to five days. I had no idea about such a project, so I had a lot to learn. I absolutely had no idea about the place, no idea of the roads or directions at all. I was like an alien out of a spaceship that landed in a place called Goa. I got on with the job. I went to see the ships in the morning with some friends. The general consensus was that it would take about five lakhs to repair the boats, but I had my doubts. I called the owner of a shipyard, who was making some equipment for my friend. He came and had a look, and in his opinion, it could take a little more.

I was visiting government authorities like crazy to collect data on tourism and boats. I visited the office of the Captain of Ports since he was the ultimate authority on water affairs. I met him and asked about the boats. He mentioned that the hull required repairs, as if I even knew what the word *Hull* meant. I heard *skull* instead of *hull* and I promptly said, 'We have already inspected the skull, sir. We shall take care of that.' I asked him if there was anything else, and he said, 'No. Otherwise, they are good.' I could go ahead with them. I was very happy I got some authority who endorsed the boats. A lot of other information was also gathered by me in the meanwhile.

The boats had been running in Goa for the last eighteen years, and Mrs. Indira Gandhi once sailed on it.

The boat had been carrying about 250 passengers when the bridge on the Mandovi had collapsed. There were still pending dues on the vessels, and so on. Tender was opening the day after, but I had to procure a form. By this time, I was excited and wanted that tender to come to only me. I went to the DOT office and somehow found out they had printed only ten forms. This was on Friday and on Monday, at two o'clock tender was to open. I bought all ten. Since the office was closed on Saturday and Sunday. Even if somebody took a form on Monday, they would need to make a demand draft and meet other terms and conditions, it would be difficult for any superstar to accomplish all these. I was standing near the counter on Monday till 12:30 p.m. Nobody else came, so most probably, I was the only person who applied for it. Anyway, I was awarded at 3:00 p.m. a three-year lease extendable every three years for three years each. In the evening, we celebrated with wine, the Goan way. I was relieved. At least the project was on. Now, I had to set the ball rolling. I needed a transport to start with and a place to live. My friend had sent a man for an interview the next morning. During the interview, I realized his qualification was his new Chetak scooter. In his mind, he was a fifth class student; but physically, he was an overgrown figure. His scooter got him the job as a manager in my company. So from a new Opel to a new Chetak, I must have sat on a scooter after two decades. The last time was probably in college. I took it as starting from scratch, a new beginning.

My friend was staying in Defence Colony, obviously because of his father. He also had his office in the same colony. It was a bungalow on a thousand yards of land, with two rooms on the ground floor. He asked me if I could take one room on rent and share the rent with him. I went there; it was no less than a junkyard. All their junk from their unsuccessful venture of a restaurant was lying there, from tandoor and tabletops to chairs and so on. Anyway, I took it, and it had two single beds without mattresses with different heights.

At least, I had an address to be printed on the letterheads. I met the landlord and his wife very casually, who mentioned an incident in the past. She said one morning she opened the door, and a black cobra was sitting right in front of the main door. She advised me to just be a little careful as there were snakes. I yelled, 'What! You mean inside the premises of the bungalow?'

I couldn't clear the mess that was lying in the drawing room, but the room certainly needed atmosphere cleaning. I would chant 'Om Namahshivaya' and go to sleep. I was also sent a servant by this friend of mine. What a character, he was a Christian and joined me one afternoon. Around 10:30 in the evening, this chap came into my room, took off his trousers, hung them on the window, and lit a bidi while preparing his bed in my room. I asked, 'Carmahlo, what are you doing? Why don't you sleep in the next room?' He said he would sleep with me because he was scared. I mean acceptance also has a limit. Finally, I managed to convince him and pushed him out of my room.

Having him in my room, was probably worse than having a Cobra. The next morning, he asked me that bread and butter needed to be bought. I gave him Rs. 50.

He showed up after an hour. I was dying for a cup of tea. He came, and I didn't have the heart to ask why he was late, so quickly I told him to make tea. He said, 'You have to give me Rs. 12'. 'For what?' I asked. He said, 'Twenty-six for your butter and bread and so on, and for thirty-six, I had breakfast. I can't have this bread for breakfast.' I was stunned with his strange behaviour.

The next morning, I came across a young guy of about twenty-three years, with ruffled hair, lost in his thoughts. He was waiting. I was told that he lost his bag in his journey and had no money. He looked like a decent guy to me. In any case, I was in the recruitment phase of operation. I interviewed him, and he had a very sad story. He had no father and mother; they died in an accident. He had to get his sister married and all. To cut the long story short, I gave him some money and asked him to join and stay with me. He occupied the next room. His name was Vicky. I told him to get ready and go to work immediately.

We went to the tourism office since we were awarded the tender. I asked for the papers of the vessels. They gave me an authority letter for GTDC to collect the papers from them as they used to manage the boats. We went to the GTDC office and kind of ransacked the office, but to no avail. We got some papers, but they were of no use. There were no registration papers of ownership, no survey reports—basically, no papers at all.

It was revealed by the GM GTDC that the boats were gifted to them by the Maharashtra government. Whatever it was, I immediately sat down in a restaurant to write a letter to the tourism that in the absence of any paper, we were not interested in the boats. I had a chat with the director of tourism, and he assured me that there was nothing wrong. These were matters of the government and would be solved immediately. He fixed a meeting with the chief minister to resolve the issue.

It was me, the MD GTDC, the COP (commissioner of ports), the Director of Tourism, the Secretary in Inland waterways, and the Chief Secretary. The meeting went very well, and everything was resolved in our favour. The Chief Secretary mentioned that tourism was our priority sector and that everyone else should see to it that these boats ran without hassle. We then took possession of one boat, *Malvika*. The other was named *Radhika*. I named my company after my elder son,

Kshitij Marine Club, or KMC. The project was on, but a lot was to be done. All of a sudden, before I realized it, I had two marine vessels, three staff, a bungalow to live, and a company registered in Goa; and it was only three weeks that I had been there with no clear ideas about the place and the people. I was told that social acceptance was a bit of a question mark with outsiders. There was this park outside my house and a swing under an old tree, right in front of my main gate. I went there very often and sat on the swing and did Satsang alone, but now I had one fellow to listen to the Bhajan and even sometimes join me.

My mind could not be stopped, and emotions were not leaving me that easily. Now that I knew that I had to live in Goa, I thought that with my past, it was going to be very difficult to live here, but my mind at that point was wreaking havoc, so it came to me that the old had to die, but how? One day, I dug a grave in the park and buried the old Abhay Khemka whom I knew personally. This event gave me a lot of peace later on. Initially, I was crying a lot, but once I buried that personality, my mind gradually started accepting my new life, as it was now easy to make my mind understand that the old had died.

I worked with the knowledge that the mind needs proof, Pranama, as Patanjali described, and slowly started to loosen my tight grip on the fiasco that had happened two months ago with me. The only time I would feel troubled was when my family would call and get totally emotional over the phone and trigger my emotional pain bodies as well. Soon I realized this phenomenon.

Let's say I was Okay, and then one of these phone calls would come through, full of emotions, and I would be miserable afterwards. I was getting sucked with the emotions. I realized that thoughts come and go. I am okay up to the time that I don't get caught up, and then I become the emotion. Then my whole being is in pain.

Guruji mentioned that emotion has a life of two days, three hours, and thirty-eight seconds. I realised that when you lose awareness and get caught up, you become a victim of emotion.

And when it has a life, meaning it is not permanent, it means it is useless. What purpose does it really solve? It comes as a tornado and sweeps me with it. Similarly, I may be doing the same thing to my folks in Delhi. They may be all right, and then I call and make them miserable. With emotions, if you look at them, they drop.

Another technique is practicing Sudarshan Kriya, a set of breathing patterns. If it is done for ten minutes, the thought process changes. To change a thought, you change your breathing pattern, and then you will see that the thought changes also. I realised that living my past is not going to give me anything but pain, so I had to forget the past. I started living in this awareness, but honestly, sometimes I would get swallowed by negative emotions, primarily in the beginning, the past and the future. The mind doesn't get dissolved that fast. It's very clever; the ego doesn't want it to happen. Their position is in jeopardy; they were the master of me and the now.

I was trying to be their master; they wouldn't allow it to happen. The intellect also joined them. The arguments were mostly won by the mind, ego, and intellect. It was like the big dog fighting the small dog inside me. Usually, the bigger dog would win, but the smaller dog was also finding ways to give a fight. Every day we would go to the COP's office asking for permission to tow the vessel to the yard for repairs. For ten days he kept telling us to furnish some papers. My season was getting marred with each passing day. He would do it in a way that one could really get frustrated, never taking any decision.

He asked us to get the vessel insured, which was alright. The next day he told us to get certified staff to man the vessel. We found certified staff somehow, but then he asked how they could be on a vessel which was not registered. Then he said that the trawler which would tow the vessel also had to be insured by us— meaning a never-ending story. Finally, out of sheer frustration, we decided that we would just tow it. Vicky managed two fishing trawlers. The trawler guy asked us which yard to take. I had no idea what a shipyard looked like. The only thing I had seen before was the Maruti service station in Delhi.

I didn't even know where the damn yards were. We pretended to be pros and asked him which would be the nearest from the Mandovi. He told us to try one on the Zuari River. Anyway, the towing started, and we were in the car and tried to reach Zuari River, which was thirty-five kilometres by road from the Mandovi. The vessel had to travel by sea and then enter Zuari.

We waited in Zuari for a long time, almost four hours, but didn't see the vessel. I was slightly getting jittery. Around seven, the vessel arrived. I tried to go to the yard people and talk to them. The vessel was about less than a kilometre from the shore, and the trawler guy came and said that he would anchor the vessel and that tomorrow only he could take it to the yard. Meanwhile, I fixed up with a yard that knew my friend. He also said it was okay for tomorrow. The next day, high tide was at 5:00 p.m., and these guys went for some reason. I was at home. By 11:00 p.m., Vicky called and said she was grounded and had hit the bottom. I told him to forget English and tell me what happened.

He explained the boat was hit hard and got stuck in the mud. Water entered, and the engine room was also submerged. My instinctive reaction was to tell him to go back home. He asked why. I said because we had to run away from there immediately as he had sunken a vessel belonging to the government.

I didn't know what to say. The next morning, we were frantically calling salvation agencies. They gave some weird quotes. This was a steel-body vessel weighing a thousand tonnes, and with water inside, another fifty tonnes. It was a gigantic task. The engine driver went into the water and entered the engine room. When he came out, he developed rashes on his body because of oil slick in the engine room. Yard guys and locals were all giving advice. Water was entering the engine room. We couldn't reach anywhere. A day passed. People were on the job with sub pumps to suck the water out, but the inflow was greater than the outflow. With the mud at sea level, the boat was sitting down by the minute.

I didn't know what to do. I told Vicky, 'Look, I am going to Meditate. You all try. This vessel can't sink. My Guru has asked me to go to Goa and do this project. If the end would be like this, he wouldn't have asked me to do it in the first place.' I told him to do Satsang with me. The next morning, we went to the yard while singing Bhajans. Fear was not there. I was filled with faith. Vicky was flabbergasted and shocked with my behaviour. The next day, nothing happened still. I went back home in the evening. He stayed back.

I sat in meditation and was praying till 2:00 p.m. In the evening he called, 'Sir, good news. She has just popped up on her own. Nobody knows how, but she is sailing.' My reaction was, it was bound to happen. He added that Guruji had done the trick. They towed it to the nearest yard, and it was kept outside the yard. The vessel was to be kept in dry dock.

I was told by the yard engineer he didn't know how they would do it. When the tide was at its highest, they could take the boat in. I was told that high tide was after three days. Meanwhile, we were somehow able to located the technician who had been looking after these engines for years. He came and checked the engines. He said that the engines had been in seawater for too long and there was only a bleak chance that they would run. Seawater could have done damage, but if and only if, they cracked at first ignition, then he could save them. I said they would crack at first ignition, so he shouldn't worry. 'You tell me what has to be arranged.' Two days later, we all gathered. The engine mechanic was also surprised by my reaction. He thought I was mad. He kept saying our attempt might be futile. I told him to go ahead; nothing was wrong with the engines. This vessel was blessed. He started the ignition, and it started going *tak-tak-tak-tak* and finally cracked. Everybody was shocked but happy. I could see that Guru was with me. His grace was being received. I said, 'Jai Guru Dev'. They took the vessel into the yard on dry dock. The belly was as big as what you would see above sea level. I was startled. I told myself, *What have you got yourself into?*

It was a huge vessel. How much steel would it consume? The yard engineer started determining how much steel it would require. The weird estimation started with money.

Meanwhile, I hired a marine engineer and also started learning about vessels. The repair job started in full swing. Although we didn't know where to buy what, gradually the yard people helped us a lot. We would be in the yard most of the time, sometimes until two o'clock early in the morning. There were shells in the hull. We had to hire two trucks just to take the shells away. Everything one would touch would fall off. The extent of corrosion was immense. I didn't have that kind of money. Early estimation was about four lakhs for each vessel. I thanked God that I only had one vessel. I called my brother in Delhi for money, and he was shocked and surprised. He asked me if I knew what I was doing. 'Your estimations have no backbone. It slips like loose tongues.'

I didn't know exactly how much the vessel would require. I told him to prepare the money against my PPF, my life savings. A surveyor was appointed for each vessel for the fitness test before it could sail. **Our COP would** not appoint a surveyor. The ministry was also putting pressure on him, but he would tell me to return the next day with additional papers. Luckily, he went on leave, and the deputy COP was there. Somehow, I made the Commissioner of Inland Waters call him to appoint a surveyor. It was a Japanese surveyor company. He told us to carry out the repairs and call him once we were finished. After fifteen days, we called him.

Everybody was tense. Nevertheless, he started hammering with his axe all over the place. He would get inside every small nook and corner with his hammer. He went into the belly and put a hammer on the lower deck. The whole lower deck fell. From the top it looked okay, but from the inside, one little hammer and to our shock, the whole lower deck collapsed. He gave us a long list of things to be done and would come after I finished all of them. For me, it was as if the heavens had fallen on me. Firstly, I was losing season time. Secondly, I didn't have enough funds to make the repairs. The whole process of laying out the lower deck again required big money. Anyway, thanks to my brother, who somehow arranged for it and sent it to me.

Every evening, Vicky and I would plan. We had some great planning sessions. We were having a ball.

We planned the repairs first, then the decoration of the bar and the restaurant on the lower deck, with both decks made of wood, just to give it a rich look. We, fortunately, found a Rajasthani carpenter also. Woodwork was also going on simultaneously. Just to place the new wooden fender cost a large amount, which was not part of the plan. The safety equipment personnel told to us through the surveyor that it was as though we would save the customers of other vessels also.

Finally, the surveyor came and checked everything and said we did a good job. 'Yours would probably be the safest vessel now on the Mandovi.' We were relieved. Since the vessel was still under the name of the Maharashtra government, the COP would not register the vessel unless it had a survey report, drawings, and so on.

All the drawings and other paper work were more or less complete from our side. For the survey report, you had to sail with the surveyor to test the stability, anchorage, safety, engine pressure, and so on, for that required certified staff. When we would go with the certificate of the staff, he would ask the staff how they could join an unregistered vessel and sail from Zuari to the Mandovi River. He would cancel their license ultimately. All our efforts were to no avail for him. After we fully repaired the vessel and spent a huge amount of money, the COP would have a technical problem in registering the boat. He challenged me that I couldn't sail on Goa waters. As an outsider, I felt no social acceptance at all, which I had known by now. Once

during a meeting, he was getting hotheaded and angry.
I told him, 'Sir, please don't bother yourself so much'.

If it had to sail it would. 'Why are you spoiling your health
for nothing? And there is no need for any challenge.
Let's just wait and see what happens. Otherwise, I
will go back. That's all.' He kept quiet. I was trying to
mobilize the ministry with regard to the registration
issue. Finally, the COP put his foot down and said until
the original papers of registration from the Maharashtra
government came, he couldn't do anything, and this
would take at least four to five months. I had planned
my inauguration on 28 February. It was 22 February
already, and still the entire lower deck had to be
repaired along with other things, and then the entire
wooden panelling had to be fixed on both decks.

A lot of work was happening. About fifty workers were
on it, from technical to woodwork. Simultaneously, a
list of invites was being finalized, and invitation cards
went into printing on the twenty-sixth. Preeti also flew
from Delhi for the function. I delivered the cards to all
the ministers. They were all happy and agreed to come.

Even CM agreed to come. The who's who of Goa were
to be there. I even invited the COP to the function,
and he agreed to come. One team was also involved
in the preparation of the party, the hiring of a music
system, lights, carpets, chairs, caterer on board, even
tandoor on board—everything was being arranged. We
were very busy but very excited at the same time. The
people at the yard were also informed that we would
take the vessel in the afternoon of the twenty-eighth.

The engine driver and the master were prepared along with other crew members. We had also kept the entire crew on payroll; they were all ready, prepared by me.

As if I was short of surprises and bad luck, this one came along in the morning of the twenty-eighth. Meanwhile, I had transferred to a bungalow in Dona Paula on the twenty-ninth. Vicky was to transfer later. It was a very nice place. We got up in the morning with the cell phone ringing as if there was no tomorrow. The first call was from the Minister of Inland Waterways. 'Hey, Abhay, what are you doing? Have you seen the newspaper? Come and see me immediately.' And he cancelled his commitment to come to the inauguration. I called for the papers. It was the surprise of my life, front page, in bold letters, and almost half the page about another illegal vessel on the Mandovi.

The information behind article was probably provided by the COP. It had the entire technical manual of the vessel and other formalities to ply. In a nutshell, it said it was a five-star-facility vessel for the Mandovi but it was illegal and unsafe. With this bad publicity of my vessel, I must have some received forty phone calls. After that, everyone cancelled their attendance to the programme.

I landed at the Secretariat at 10:00 a.m. sharp in the concerned Minister's chamber, along with the director of DOT. There were a lot of questions. They asked how I could go on. Preeti was with me. She broke into tears and pleaded with the Minister. 'What is our fault? It was your tender. If the government is not the legitimate owner, then why tender the vessel? And they were running for over eighteen years in Goa without any papers. Then why is it a big deal now? We have spent a fortune on repairs to get the vessel ready. What is the hassle? And all that to no avail.'

The whole thing went flat like a Diwali firecracker that didn't burn after it caught fire. Mark, my only friend, had also come to discuss the partnership percentage last week, and he demanded equal partnership, but he would neither work nor put in any finances. However, he would protect me from the Mafia. We had a heated argument, and I told him to give me the same terms and I'd go back to Delhi, although when I had asked him, in the beginning he had refused any partnership. He said, 'It's your project, and I want nothing'.

But I had already given him 5 percent of the profits and there was no loss for him. Anyway, misfortune never comes alone. This fellow made a phone call to the landlord and asked him to tell me to vacate the house by 12:00 pm the same day.

The landlord called and told me to vacate the place. My explanation didn't convince him. I also gave up and agreed to vacate the place. I had nothing much with me but to vacate on a two-hour notice. Since he had come on so strongly, instead of taking the vessel out of the yard, I took myself out of the house. One could not imagine how things could change in a day. Seriously, there was a lot at stake for me. The meetings with the Ministry and the article in the newspaper made we feel that probably I had reached the end of the road. The Goa chapter was over for me. I had nowhere to run.

Most of my things I had stuffed in my car. The 'Rest',I asked Vicky to sell off and give salaries to everyone, including himself, and the balance he should send back to me to Delhi. Vicky told me, 'Since nothing can be done now, sir, you leave. You have had enough. This place is not worth living for you.'

As we were parting our ways, we both had tears in our eyes. We left everything and went to Preeti's mother's house in Pune, with the boat in the yard finally ready to sail.

As we started our journey to Pune, both of us had tears flowing, but we were doing Satsang in the car. All Art of Living bhajans.

All of a sudden, we managed to escape an accident. There was this sharp turn that I took. One side was down the mountain. I managed to take the car to the right. There was this truck coming from the other side. Somehow, thank God we escaped. Our tears suddenly dried up. There was silence for some time. I told Preeti, 'If we had to crash, this was it. God is there. We are not going down like this for nothing. God has different plans, it seems.' Anyway, we reached Pune at about 9:00 p.m.

With no face to show to anybody we arrived, they were all surprised to see us. My brother-in-law came and asked me what went wrong. I told him there was still some time left. 'Let's wait and see what happens. Let destiny take its course. God decides now. Whatever is his decision shall be accepted by me.' What other alternative was there for me in life? I had no other option but to accept the happenings, such was my state. We were discussing this, and meanwhile, a phone call came on my mobile. 'Hello, I am CM's Secretary. CM wants to see you tomorrow in his office.' I asked, 'The day after will do?'. He said okay.

We were in Goa the next day. I was going through the motions. There were no expectations, no curiosity, no anxiousness. I met the CM. He was very nice. He assured me he would set things in order. He directed me to meet the Chief Secretary, who would do what was necessary. I checked in a hotel as I had left the house I had on lease. I called the staff.

One should have seen their faces. The Chief Secretary was from North India and was very helpful. The COP was called and asked to register the boat with whatever papers were available or without papers if need be.

In spite of this, he insisted that they required the original ownership documents from Bombay, but this time, he was a little mild in his approach and appeared to be doing what was required. I had viral fever and was down. A little bit of woodwork on the boat was still pending, so I called the contractor or carpenter. He saw an opportunity and started blackmailing for more money. Luckily, I used to visit a North Indian cuisine restaurant run by North Indian youth, whose uncle was DIG in the Goa police. The carpenter was set right.

I had an old friend from Delhi who was living close by. He offered me to stay in his house until we found a place. I declined in the beginning, but on Preeti's and his insistence, I agreed. There were also now funds required, but guess what, my share broker's wife called for the outstanding balance I had with them. Although I had paid the rest, I asked her for more time and couldn't explain my condition. As she was coming strongly and crying and giving all sorts of sob stories, I told her my inability to pay didn't make me a bad guy. I would arrange something shortly. Probably she was also under a lot of pressure. I called Vicky, who had also been down with malaria for the last few days. I came to know he was now all right but was not coming to see me. This was strange. My staff member told me that the day I had left for Pune, he had seen Vicky with a few guys in Tito's nightclub ordering tequila shots.

I met Vicky. He admitted that he sold all the stuff and had a nice time with the money. Somehow I couldn't control myself and slapped him real hard. This was the end of him in my organization.

We transferred to a new house in a couple of days, and things started looking good again. The Australian cricket team was there for a day in Goa. I tied up with sponsors, and they agreed to have the team on our vessels. The COP, as usual, denied this agreement and said that formalities were still not completed. The sponsor was pretty upset. All arrangements went haywire. The COP's reaction was very upsetting and frustrating. I told God to help him please. He was collecting a lot of negative karma. He was still continuing with his ifs and buts, and I was putting more money in the project. He was becoming a real pain in the ass.

The question of whether the project would take off or not was still on. When the COP said no, I recall telling him, 'Sir, my bad times are over and my good times are on, but your bad times are round the corner'. He kept his mouth shut. After this, there was silence in the room. The yard meter was on and really shooting up. The vessel had been in the yard for a very long time now. All budgets were going haywire. Funds were becoming a scarce commodity. These were really dark days. I was always in a catch-22 situation and didn't know what to do.

Suddenly, on Good Friday I received a call from the COP at 8:00 a.m. asking me to come to his house in next half an hour promptly. I went there.

His office was closed. It was a holiday in Goa. He took me to his office, searched my file, signed a paper, and gave it to me. I nearly jumped out of my chair. It was a permission to ply on a temporary region. Christians say that on Good Friday, change of heart takes place. The COP then chatted with me for over two hours. He told me all his history, his childhood and so on. I was 'flabbergasted'. It was some change of heart. We were all jumping. Now the project was on sure. I was so relieved.

One the next tide, which was in a day or so, we took the vessel out and brought it to the Mandovi river finally.

At the jetty, we were given permission to ply alongside GTDC's boat *Santa Monica*, where they had plied for years in the past. Much to my surprise, GTDC did not allow us to dock. After a hue and cry, we were allowed to dock.

I started my business on 13th of May, my Guruji's birthday. We had a Satsang on the boat. My entire Art of Living family in Goa had been called. It was simply amazing. Bhajans were probably reaching all parts of Goa with a twenty-thousand-watt music system on board. The next cruise was full. It was very heartening. The Guru's grace was pretty evident, but the off season in Goa was immediately awaiting us, which started June onwards. I tied up with a bus operator so that a fixed number of customers were ensured, but he said he would give me INR 50,000 a month. All expenses would be borne by him. I agreed as I had no other option, and also I was desperate to go back to Delhi for some time.

I guess I was tired. But when I came back, I didn't get any money from him. I also came to know that he was connected with notorious people.

I concentrated on the season ahead instead of wasting time with him. I was happy at least my staff salaries were paid barring some amounts. We did some extensive marketing with five-star hotels. We got a lot of tie-ups also, but my competitors had different plans for me. They got united and with the COP planned to take the docking away from me. We landed in the middle of the Mandovi River. Their timing was perfect in the beginning of the season. I got busy in mobilizing the Secretariat. After a month of efforts, I got the order from the COP to dock in the same place again. CM was again instrumental in this. Thanks to him, I got the order and went to dock my vessel, but GTDC denied my docking and phoned the police. The police came, and I was picked up by them and landed at the police station. He seemed to have been influenced by the GTDC Chairman. He warned me not to do such things in the future. I asked him, 'Sir, do what? I have the written orders. I am the complainant. I had filed a complaint in your office earlier.' But that's Goa. I went to all the authorities but to no avail again. Every morning I would sit in the Secretariat. Everybody started recognizing me, as if I was working there and not visiting. I would enter without any pass now.

All marketing efforts went in vain. It was January again, CM came to my rescue, and this time around, he decided to give me a berth or dock in another jetty close by. This reminds me of a very funny incident. I went in CM's room, and there were the Minister, the COP, and the Chief Secretary. It was full of high officials. They were discussing my case, but I was singing Bhajans inside me, totally oblivious to what was happening. This is one incident where I witnessed consciousness with no concept in mind, no expectation, just being in the now, in the present moment.

They gave orders to transfer my boat to another jetty, setting up another place to operate from, however there was no regular tourist traffic there. The Mandovi jetty was known for cruising, but not this one. In a way, I thought this would be better, at least no fights. One could operate peacefully. There was no light on the jetty, so we applied and requested jetty officials to give as connection. We were denied, but at the same time, CM inaugurated floodlights at the other jetty to promote tourism in the state. So we took a lead from the boat's generator, but the hassle was that whenever the boat would leave, the lights would also leave. We used to tell the passengers that the electricity had gone, however the business continued to drop. As if this was not enough, I received a phone call that Bhai of Goa, the Mafia, to let me know that he wanted to see me. We met at Kamat Hotel in Panjim, with some five to six other guys. I thought I was fortunate at least I was meeting top guns. His opening sentence was "Boss, two things are here in Goa:the sea and the jungle. If we kill a guy and throw him in the water, the fish will eat him. If we kill him and throw him in the jungle, the wild animals will eat him. Nobody will know where the man is gone."

After this, Bhai put forth his terms. He only wanted 40 percent of turnover (not the profit) to protect me from everything, and all guides/tours would also bring business if he talked to them. For a while, I thought to get up and fight and not be afraid but I chose to surrender and not perish.

I asked if I could have my coffee. I needed time to think. I finished my coffee and told Bhai that 40 percent was too little. 'Why don't you take 60 percent and give me 40 percent?' Bhai was stunned. He asked me, 'Can I finish my coffee?' And he kept mum for some time. At the same time, he was very happy. He said that 40 percent was enough but that he liked me very much.

He had not met a more endearing guy than me and assured me that I should not worry about anything.

I told myself that this meant worry for everything. His man would come every day, and we had to get the audit done. There was chaos, but because business was also dropping and we were becoming close friends, he decided to leave us after some time.

I started new things on the boat as part of my New Year's resolution. I would start the day's work with the entire staff with some breathing techniques and then hearing out their problems. All of them quite enjoyed it, including me. Then before the cruise, we would start with a Bhajan by Nitin Bhai of Art of Living. Just to see their interest, I stopped it for fifteen days. After a while, everybody came to me and requested to perform our exercise again. I knew we were getting united, and slowly a lot of internal politics went away. I saw lot of smiling faces in spite of the hardships.

Once we had a dolphin trip in the morning, and I had no money for diesel. I remember the staff managed to chip in a little money they had with them. Nobody troubled me for overtime, salary, and so on. We were working as a family and for the same cause; my staff was excellent.

Ever since I had come from Delhi in August and had transferred to a new house, I took to Sadhna very seriously and read Osho, as I had time on my side and was alone.

I would also meditate on the setting sun at Miramar beach before going to work, barring loneliness at times and no social life or anybody to share anything. I was resorting more to silence. I did an advanced course again. It was held in a nearby house. Art of Living wanted me to head the Goa chapter, but I refused. I preferred to be with myself instead of entering dirty politics that the Goa chapter had. One can say with this advanced course and regular Sadhna plus Osho's teachings, I realised a lot about the strength or power of silence. We will take this up later.

To test my Sadhana, one day I went to visit my friend. He had his Turkish girlfriend over. She was looking for a spiritual Guru in India. He said, 'Why go far? Why don't you take lessons from my friend?' She looked at me and said, 'I said spiritual Guru'. Obviously, if someone looks at me, he can say I could be anything but spiritual. Anyhow, she agreed. I started yoga with her, lying down in Shavasan Meditation. I told her we would experience a lessening of thought bombardment. After our meditation, when I asked her, 'How did you experience the no thought feeling?' she said, 'The moment you said look at the thoughts, they were bombarding me like crazy. Never stopped. Obviously, first time, no such thing happens.' Business was gradually drying up at the new jetty. We would come up with lots of schemes for hotels and guides as well as tourists, but they weren't showing signs of improvement.

Also, the MCD problems of putting up a signboard or a small hut that we had created to sell tickets plus the regular COP notices for nothing were very unproductive and non sensical things. I decided to go to Delhi. Also, I knew Guruji would be there as well. I wanted to ask him about transferring my family to Goa, as I was not happy staying alone, and Preeti and the kids were not very happy either.

I met Guruji in April, and he listened to me and Preeti. He instructed my family to be together. So we should transfer to and live in Goa together. I went back happily and started looking for schools.

The best in Goa was not even average in Delhi, but that was that. I talked to some people, and a person from my Art of Living family knew a principal and told me to come along with him to see the principal. Well, everything went well, and I was asked to deposit money for admission. It was an ICSC based school, and my kids had been in CBSE based school before, but they were sweet enough to agree and put in extra work. They were also coming to Goa on the first week of June to spend their holidays. It was a month and a couple of weeks, so I decided when they would be around, the admission procedure could be done, but one thing was hankering in my mind: the jetty was not suited for tourist activities. All competitors were also after my life. Also, business was not good, but Guruji told me to transfer my family. Things looked a little upsetting, but not for long. I received another notice from the COP to vacate the jetty.

That order didn't say where he was transferring me. It just asked me to vacate the jetty by the 16th of June.

My family was arriving the next morning. I didn't mention anything to them. They had a mind-set to change, so that's why they were going to Goa with this perspective. My younger son was in good humour after seeing the school and said, 'Papa, this! *Chalo theek hai*.' But there were no marks for guessing that it was the pits. It was evening. We were generally talking to each other. This was when I decided enough was enough. 'I am quitting this and going back', I told Preeti. She said, 'But there is a lot at stake, isn't it?' I said, 'We shall see. Any decision is good if taken.'

The next morning, I went to the DOT office and asked them to come and take over the boat, and I told them I couldn't take it home in the absence of a docking place. Their officials came. Somehow I was very happy. I talked to myself that my time in Goa was over, so instead of thinking about my loss, I was rejoicing and feeling very light, as if I was freed. I ordered some samosas and jalebis for the officials. One of them, seeing me in this mood, asked, 'Why are you so happy when you invested two years and so much money here? And honestly speaking, I know everybody has troubled you, including me.' The question was coming from his heart. I looked at him. He had tears in his eyes. I told him, 'I have nothing against you or anyone else here in Goa, not even the COP. In my movie, my coming here was essential, and you had to play this role, so you all did what was required. There is no fault of yours.

You all had to act only in this fashion, but now my good time will start, so I am happy.' The guy embraced me and promised me if he could do anything for me, I should let him know. Later on, the boat was auctioned by the Tourism Department. I found out that the vessel had been sold for pittance, out of which one fourth was received by me. The Government preferred the exchequer to remain healthy, instead of justice. I was told the rent must be paid in twenty-four months. It was immaterial whether there was docking or any other facility was provided. On the whole, the funniest was the COP had issued a fitness certificate to the same boats in 1992, and that time it wasn't also registered with them. The Goa government was not even owners of it. Also, I was there for two years.

The agreement of lease was never done. This inspired me to go to the Law **Department and file a case, but I eventually didn't.** Goa has a long way to progress. They lack some much-needed exposure. It's an overgrown village and not a state. But this time around, there was no feeling of loss. On the contrary, a feeling of contentment and fulfilment was there. No feeling of self-blame or guilt was there. No fear of tomorrow. No fear that I shut this down and would have to start all over again. What face would I show to the world? Or in a nutshell, what would happen to me? How would I manage the household and so on? For the first time I realised I had given my 100 percent. There was nothing more one could have done. The result is never in your hands, so be it. Everything happens for the good. Every downfall is for growth, and literally, I could see growth in this whole event. There was no fear, resentment, loss, or anything.

This happens when you give your 100 percent. Then where is the scope of the complaint left, blame left? One takes it as a happening and becomes a witness.

In fact, right from the beginning, when I had reached Goa and was so down with emotional, mental, and financial problems, during an introspection session, I said to myself, 'I have lost everything, so to say, but what is there that I can save which will take me to the future? Because this is my darkest period and will not remain in this situation forever. A bright sunshine will come. Nothing remains the same. Change is permanent.' But at the same time, depression was taking its toll on me. After meditation, in serenity, under a tree where I usually sat on a swing, I realised events and situations are not permanent and will change.

Also, its your dharma and karma to get up and fight. But with the state of mind that I was in, it was impossible. I was going down. The answer that came to me was in the present scenario. What I could save was my mind.

My state of mind, because that's the only thing I could save. That's the only thing which would enable me to fight back and go through the rough period. That's the only thing which would take me beyond this problematic time and situation. Problems exist. Every time you have a problem in the mind, and continuously chews on it. A small thing becomes big. That means a big thing can also become small, which means it's a state of mind, which also means you can go beyond it.

It's a question of from where you are seeing and what you are perceiving out of it. This meant crying and getting depressed was actually draining my energy, and with a poor state of mind, I was getting more depressed and things were looking gloomier. So I looked at the whole phenomenon and started to reverse the situation.

First, instead of draining my energy, I thought with Kriya Yog to enhance or gain energy. I also looked at depression carefully. There were times where I would think about it and chew on it. I would get depressed and drained, which means that depression is nothing but getting stuck in your mind with one set of thoughts. What would happen to me?Generally, fearful thoughts or thoughts coming out of fear or a fearful state of mind means if I push it slightly farther and not get stuck, I would take myself out of depression.

I had to gain energy instead of draining it. Gaining and draining energy both, I looked at. Draining, I knew how it was taking place. Gaining had to be sorted out. That was the test of all my Gyan under my belt, the so-called knowledge, but this was all stored knowledge. Now was the time to get this converted into wisdom. Knowledge on an experiential basis turns into wisdom.

The constant chattering of the mind and then getting sucked into it meant that instead of facing a problem, I was becoming the problem. I remembered the Buddha's teachings. Once the Buddha was sitting with his four disciples. He took a handkerchief and put five knots in it and then asked everyone what it was. One said it was a piece of cloth.

Another a handkerchief, knotted hanky, but the last one said a piece of cloth but now knotted. Buddha asked how to make it a hanky again. He explained you should go in the reverse order. The way you put the knots, go in the reverse, now unknot it. You achieve the original.

This was a big help for me. I realized the drain, looked at it, and went in the reverse order. Looked at the mind. It starts with a negative thought, starts to chew on it, keeps chewing, and results in depression. The drain was caused as I was going outwards because of chewing on my thoughts, instead of going inwards and meditating. That's the reverse order. You will achieve your true nature. Initially, the process was difficult, but very soon it started giving good results. And this also started my spiritual journey and journey of knowledge to wisdom in many aspects of my life.

I understood that to correct any wrongdoing, you will have to go in the reverse direction that much. Hindus have depicted this with Krishna and Radha. Krishna means the source. Radha is the reverse of Dhara (Dhara means a stream), and Radha is going in the opposite direction of the stream and reaching the source. If you go in the reverse direction of the river, you meet the source. Christ also said, 'I am the only way. I am the pure consciousness. Go back to your consciousness and you shall meet the Lord.' That's the only way; absolutely it is.

Hindus also emphasize Prayaschitta. Prayas with the Chitta turn the Chitta upside down in the reverse. Prayaschitta is important.

It is necessary to go in the reverse to balance. You have to go in the reverse direction. At the helm of every emotion there is silence. After we shout a lot, what do we do? Go into silence. After crying a lot, we go into silence. In an aftershock, we also go into silence. This is a natural defence mechanism the body, to naturally go in the reverse, but I have the theory of the useful and useless.

Useless for me is very important, although we disregard *useless* these days. *Useless* for me defines *useful*. The quality of your night's sleep defines the quality of your awakening. I say the same for rest and activity. This is why doctors even recommend that you go on vacation. Think why we feel light and nice when we are on vacation. In a new environment where nobody knows you, your ego starts to loosen its grip on you. 'I am this or that?' People know you in a certain way, so you behave according to their expectations and not according to what you are. But in a new place, the ego or identification with your mind starts to melt. You feel lighter not because you are staying in a five-star hotel or flying business class but because nobody knows you. You are now a nobody. You start to loosen up from your identity. You are away from usefulness. You have entered uselessness.

In meditation, you do the useless; in fact, meditation is nothing but dropping all actions. Not doing anything is meditation. Complete uselessness. *Useless* is at zero value. Look at the pendulum of a watch. It goes to the right side. Actually, it's gaining momentum to go to the left side. **Look at a *tightrope walker*.**

If he goes to the right side, he goes to his left side as well to balance. In the centre is the balance at zero level. If he is going to the left or right is a deviation from the balance, from zero. Actually, at zero lies the balance. **However, in life it is difficult to be on zero all the time, so you have to balance and operate like a tightrope walker.**

As Buddha said, be in the centre. Take the middle path. Any value accumulated by the mind is a mere deviation from harmony, from your true self, true nature. The sunrises only to gain momentum to set. How can a value exist in the cosmos? If a value is there, negative or positive, it will be lopsided. Then only zero can exist, can't it? Harmony or cosmic balance lies in zero. Much emphasis is laid on usefulness these days to excel right from childhood. The more you are in the useful mode, the more you will be solidifying the mind and its madness. And you start to get spent on the obsession that you are carrying. The more in control is the mind, the more it will be the boss. You have to constantly be aware of this fact and be watchful of what you are getting spent on. You don't have to get spent; you have to live. Be aware of this fact. 'What am I getting spent on?' The more the mind has control over you, the more it will drive you towards madness, towards obsession.

Actually, if you go back to the definition of usefulness, *useless* will not allow complete control of you by the mind, and therefore, the mind is kept in check. You will then not be obsessed or spent. If you keep watching your breath and the silence of the subconscious, you will be driving this mind to loosen its grip on you.

You will gradually start to become its boss rather than its slave. Unless you are aware of this fact, you will be spent and not live a balanced life. If you are not aware you are feeding the monster inside you, the result can only be disastrous. Insanity can only prevail.

Usually, we hear, 'Increase awareness'. Increase awareness to unawareness. To the monster mind, awareness is about what, how to be aware of what. See if you are acting out of emotions. You have to be aware if you are acting out of your five sensory elements—touch, taste, sight, smell, and ego—or an obsessed monster, recognising that nothing coming out of the mind is ever of any great consequence. Only sorrow and misery, and they make you remain in the opposite polarity zone. And if you are aware of this fact, then you are on the right track.

Terms like acceptance and surrender, how do you achieve them? Actually, once a person has recognized the mind and is operating with this new state of mind, which is devoid of emotions and obsessions, one can't help but be in total acceptance of what is, with the whole, with one's own rhythm and the cosmos. Then surrender is the natural outcome. It's wonderful. Now the bigger mind is taking all decisions. They can only be good for you, just for you, for your higher self. Growth can happen. Surrender is now the natural outcome. Otherwise, it's the way you have arranged the mind, which will not last, which is temporary, and which will not help. If it is done with effort, so to say with mental makeup, that I have to surrender, then it's with effort, and then it's manipulation, and then it is simple compromise.

You have given in. It will not sustain and might not be recommended if you have to exist in this world.

See, with this state of mind, where you recognize the mind and don't allow it to interfere with your actions, the action by itself is of higher good. I will cite an example. See, if a man is happy and in a good state of mind, you will never hear, he has picked up a dagger and murdered someone, so if someone is resorting to murder, obviously, he is not in a state of happiness. Similarly, if you are in a state of depression, you can't do any act which will win you a noble prize.

You start acting from subjectivity to objectivity, and that is what is required. Now a leap of faith also happens, with faith at the base. Or we can say implicit faith. Everything that you require or want to get done happens just before you actually require it. It's amazing how the cosmos or divine takes care of you and your needs. You are completely taken care of. You can now put your car or life in neutral and enjoy. Now the punter has finally learnt this.

Generally, we are all brought up in a typical household setup. We grow up seeing our parents working, in business, or so to say, chasing money with no real goal in the mind. In the garb of insecurity and social structure such as ours, nothing is more. Much is still less. We don't know where to put a full stop. There is no respite, no cool off, no stopping. Just die collecting for the next generation. Much emphasis is on doing things which are useful only. *Useless* is thrown out of the window, system, and society at large. The reverse never happens.

That's why problems remain even in the affluent class. You can't go in only one direction. The reverse is as important as the forward march. The cosmos has a perfect balance in everything.

Look at day and night, birth and death. That's why they say change is permanent. You can't go in any one direction. You believe as much as you doubt. Otherwise, why do you need to believe? Truth is truth. It doesn't require belief or doubt. If it does, then it's not truth. We have lost God in this mind game of belief and doubt and complicated things around us. Belief and doubt have no meaning but values created out of the mind. Actually, you believe in the same quantity as much as you doubt. Truth being at zero value is beyond all this. The sun is there. The mountain is there. No belief, no doubt. It is there. That's the truth. The biggest renunciatory are those who chased money all their lives. They have to strike a balance and come at zero. Otherwise, they will go mad. There will be no peace. To attain peace, they give everything in the end and come at zero. This is the law of nature. Buddha tells us to take the middle path. **Any value created by the mind is a mere deviation from the harmonized axis.**

Naturally, for me, Prayaschitta happened in this Goa venture. I knew some punishment (self-imposed) should be there, for putting my family in a problem for my rash and irresponsible act of dabbling into the share market, but in retrospect, I believe I had done my Prayaschit. Now, I have done a lot of meditation and Kriya Yog. Apart from this, at least a thousand hours of listening to Osho's tapes.

'Whenever a caterpillar thinks it is dying, it turns into a butterfly.'

I was back in Delhi in June 2002, going back to my office daily. I was taking stock of my own self, but one thing was clear: I was twenty times stronger in my mind than when I had gone to Goa. I didn't have any hangovers of the past. I had understood the knots were opened, and the original hanky was back. Going in the reverse holds a lot of solutions to life situations.

You don't spend your life span chasing a single axis. You simply watch it happen. You allow a bigger mind to take control of you. Surrender happens automatically. You are in the safe hands of the Almighty. You start to see and accept things which come naturally to you, rather than interfering with your small mind and changing the course of what nature/cosmos wants to give. You are then cut off from the whole cosmic setup. You are on your own. You can't remain safe in this situation for a long time. The sum total then will have to be zero. When the cosmos gives, that is what is natural, what you deserve, what is due to you based on your karma.

One Art of Living teacher once came to me to take some advice. He had three offers from three different companies in the UAE. He asked which one to take. 'I can't decide', I said. 'You like the one that is giving you the best package'. He said, obviously, 'What do you say?' I told him, 'It's not you who is deciding. It's your greed who is deciding.

Anything greed decides can't be the best for you. You wait. See which one nature wants to give you. Which comes naturally to you is the best for you.'

Our small mind can only see through our needs and greed, and that can't be the right choice. In greed the mind stops to work. The intellect stops to work. Only greed works. A bigger mind always gives you the best, what you deserve, what is good for your higher self. I told him to wait for the offer rather than choosing. When I met him a couple of months later, he mentioned he was very happy with his job, which finally had come to him naturally without chasing anyone.

I had earlier said that every emotion has a corresponding breathing pattern; therefore, if we have harmonised breathing, then there shall be no emotion. Then you don't get caught up with emotions and lead a life based on emotions. Emotion then is nothing but a deviation from a harmonised breathing pattern or a deviation from your axis, which means that emotions have no value, just a deviation from the axis.

On the axis rests your true nature, which is peace. The natural outcome of peace is love, and then bliss comes out. Then bliss is nothing but a natural outcome. You then don't do things seeking joy out of them. Your action is then an expression of joy. Emotion is generated out of your perception or projection of your mind, and the mind has a quality to only complicate things. It can't keep things simple. Being simple means the egoistic mind dies.

The ego can't let that happen. If you look at it this way, you will be looking at it objectively rather than getting engaged and living out of emotions. Emotions will come, but you have to be aware of them so that you are not sucked by them. You have to keep balancing by looking at it. It will gradually loosen its grip. You just have to watch it. Not getting caught up with it holds the key. Watching it holds the key. Being aware holds the key. Ashtavakra tells you to be a witness. Buddha tells you to watch your breath. Don't do anything else. If you are aware and keep watching your breath, witnessing automatically happens. Then you are on the path towards freedom.

Then the bigger mind can do things for you, which are best for you. This is what I call dropping of the mind, getting out of your own way. Then nature takes control of you. The word *Dropping* holds the key. See, we talked about the mind, which can't be treated at the level of the mind. Anything you resist will persist because you resist with the mind. You can't do it for long. You can tell your mind not to get angry, but you are managing your mind. You are manipulating it. You can't do it for long. It's like sweeping dust under the carpet. It's an arrangement you have done. It can't be for the long term. It will come up again.

It's like someone did this experiment: They kept twenty youths away from girls for three months. They thought they had forgotten sex, but the moment these guys came in contact with girls, they were back to normal. People also renounce sex like many other things. This sort of leaving is not going to help. It's an arrangement.

It's manipulating the mind. Look, sex has to leave you and go.

You can't leave it. You may deny it for some time— that's all. Once you have seen the futility it has and looked at it objectively, desire can also drop by the experience of it, and you have experienced enough to come to understanding the futility. It may leave you and go. That's dropping it naturally. The rest remains to be manipulation.

These days, youths follow another arrangement of living in. Instead of seeking marriage, they feel that marriage generally doesn't work. See, marriage was an arrangement of the mind. Living in will also be an arrangement, but after a while, this will also not work.

I have seen a lot of sages on TV. They all talk about controlling the mind, and even when they talk of surrender, acceptance, and so on, all these are at the level of the mind. They are mostly telling you to change the arrangement. That's why I see people involved in spirituality and have gained nothing, because they are talking about subjectivity. They will also engage you in past life karma and heaven in the future. You are engaged in the past and the future. Nothing is going to change. Much of spirituality is on an imaginary axis and full of subjectivity, like many previous births Karma shall be washed in meditation. Nothing is happening in this birth. What previous birth are you talking about? I have a problem now. Give me a solution now. Tell me how to do it, a solution which works, not drop it. It's not going to happen, meaning you have to do this or that to control it. Any of this or that is managing your mind, but it will then exist.

It will not drop. The ego doesn't allow it to happen. Then the death of the mind will take place. The ego will not allow this. On the contrary, it will complicate it further. It loves complications. In simplicity it dies. It can't tolerate this.

Probably, the whole purpose of writing this book is you will not get these answers anywhere. How can you drop the mind? With effort you get into another arrangement. That's all. Nothing will change. You may keep chasing your Gurus forever. There are many options of Gurus these days. People are also following them left, right, and centre. But who has achieved anything so far but the Guru? They are telling you to do this or that. It's of no use, believe me. You can't achieve anything.

Everybody has seven chakras, seven energy centres. On each energy centre, opposite values exist, for example, at the base of spine: enthusiasm, inertia, and inaction exist. Behind the genitals: lust and creativity exist. On the navel: greed, jealousy, and magnanimity exist. On the heart: love, hate, and fear exist. On the throat: culture and sadness exist. In between your eyebrows: anger and awareness exist, that is called the the third eye as well. Now, we can all follow this simple phenomenon of changing values from *negative* to *positive* by meditating on the relevant chakra, and you would have some excellent results.

For instance, if you have lusty thoughts troubling you, you can indulge yourself in some creative activity. You would see lust gone. See, in love, lovers have no fear.

They often talk about dying for their loved ones. I will jump from the mountain for you and so on. They even retaliate and do things against the social norms without fear of anything.

Also, there is another way of looking at it. When love happens with the mind, just know that hate is around the corner because your love has come out of the mind, not your natural self, because you are not at your natural self. You are in the mind. You have no experience of your natural self. Love exists at the giving end, not at the receiving end, and it's a big indication. If you are in love and the other person is at the receiving end, consider that love is coming out of the mind. Look at the love of Radha, Meera, or Gopies. They were all at the giving end, and that's why it's called the highest form of love, unconditional. Otherwise, love will perish. The opposite will take place.

Opposites are complementing, what is hate. It can't exist without love, so it's a distorted form of love, nothing else. It's the opposite value, that's all. But only love exists because your basic self is love. Hate is only love gone in the opposite direction.

See, awareness and anger. In anger there is no awareness. You just want to do things which you can't even comprehend in awareness. But if you are aware, you will not get angry at all. When you know about something, then you don't get angry, do you? After anger, repentance comes, because repentance is the opposite value of anger. So neither anger nor repentance has any meaning.

People on both values get emotional, instead of being objective about it. That anger came, which means that repentance will shortly follow. If you look at it, both are useless. Later on, anger and repentance don't get caught with emotions coming out, but see, both are useless. And this only happens because you lost awareness, so put things straight. Bring in awareness rather than getting caught up in your emotion. That's why I say emotion has no value. It's only awareness lost.

To change the value, or go to the other end, you need to meditate on that chakra to change the value of that Chakra and move to the other value. Don't go to doctors. They will tell you to control your anger. How can you? You can only manage and result in increasing it. You need to drop it. That's the only Sutra. Drop naturally without effort. With effort, you can't reach anywhere. Looking at emotions objectively, being aware of your breath, and observing the silence of the subconscious, gradually you will start going beyond mind games, and the whole jigsaw puzzle will fall in its place. No effort is required.

Nobody tells you how dropping of the mind will take place without effort. A lot of people tell to control your mind. It's all in the mind; drop your mind. This also actually made me think that this doesn't work. Then how can dropping take place? Effort means creating value in some direction, either *positive* or *negative*. Basically, it's arranging or changing the arrangement. All it does is go from one arrangement to another and, after another arrangement, sometimes change as well.

The mind also has a property to prove a thing and then disprove it after a while. The mind can not accept one thing, it needs change. The ego thrives on change and complication. Another thing you will come across is controlling the ego. How can you control the ego?

I needed to go beyond this business of controlling, but I wasn't pushing it, in the manner that I wanted the answer right now. I said it should be left to the bigger mind. It should originate on its own. With effort, I can't chase a black cat in the dark. The effort is useless, stupid in nature.

Nature was to give this answer. When I say breath will initiate the process, it means an emotion has a corresponding breathing pattern. Then we start to live in a certain emotional pattern. As Patanjali said, rhythmic breathing breaks the compulsive thought pattern or emotional pattern that you are in. That's why so much emphasis was given to Pranayama in our Vedas. Do some breathing exercises. This also establishes you to your axis, where harmonised breathing takes place. *When harmonized breathing sets in you, then bombardment of thoughts is minimized, and your subconscious also settles.*

This is not talking all the time. Drainage of energy stops. For this, you also have to raise your level of awareness.

You have to practice to keep watching your breath and be with the now, the moment. Initially, you may just set right the breathing pattern. A lot of bullshit will vanish from your life. With the increase in Prana, you feel full of life and away from emotional hassles.

Actually, emotional problems also create blockages in your body. Then they solidify with time and then become a disease such as cancer, diabetes, or hypertension. Disease is nothing but being away from ease (*disease*). So come in ease, and disease will go away. Your energy centres will work/function better. Your aura will then improve. A lot of good things will happen as far as health is concerned.

Once, over a period, done regularly, your breathing is set, and you are aligned to your axis. Then start the practice of watching your breath. You would notice that when you watch your breath, the thoughts stop. When the thoughts stop, you are in the now. You are then collecting no value or karma. That's the time you start to go nearer the cosmic energy field or pure consciousness. You may even call it close to God, so the theory is simple. How much closer do you want to get that much awareness you generate? Simply, as you go closer to abundance/cosmic rhythm, your own rhythm, abundance in your life starts to flow. It's the natural outcome, no magic, no trick. You don't require anybody.

Christ, Buddha, Sant Kabir, or any other enlightened being was not chasing any Guru.

Do not try to set or change anything first. I control anger or drop the ego, or control the mind, stop chattering the mind, fulfil the desire first, be satisfied; and then I shall start and so on. These are natural outcomes. If you are closer to harmony inside, material abundance is also part of it. Don't bother about money or making money first.

Then I shall start peacefully. In fact, material abundance is a small part of the whole abundance that you can have. One will see, as we go along with the story, how things keep changing.

After leaving Goa and coming back to Delhi in 2002, I had to start from scratch again, but this time fear or pressure was not there. But also there was no work. I tried to set up a lot of things, but nothing seemed right. I contacted a very dear friend and told him about my state of affairs. He suggested a couple of things. One of them was that a common friend had opened a telephone exchange calling card, business, meaning you buy a card worth some value and you could make ISD calls at a cheaper value. I told myself if a bigger mind wants me to sell these stupid cards, then I might as well do it. I started selling them, but as luck would have it, the friend who started the business ran into trouble. One month later, I learnt he had no license to do this business. I had to sleep with fifty thousand worth of cards later on.

The friend was also underground for a while. There was no sign of him. Then one day, I was going through newspaper ads, and I came across an ad which said an exporter was required. I called them up. Some lady picked up. She was very receptive and gave me an appointment to meet her boss. This was a buying agency for Canada. On the first phone call, I told her that I was currently not in export but that I had done it for nineteen years of my life, but I had no setup. Somehow she never doubted anything and called us. I went with my brother to meet the buying agent. He was also convinced and was ready to give orders.

He gave us a few samples. Now it hit us. How would we get setup in the next seven days in export? The time frame was two to three months to execute the order. We called our old master and supervisor. Both luckily were also free, searching for a job. Both came, and soon we were back in action.

For one and a half years, this export was going fine. We were also settled in the trade, feeling that from a firm, we were becoming a company. Then came along my son's friend's father. His nephew was also importing in the USA. We met, and he had an order of some jeans shirt for the U. S. market. His nephew was also in Delhi from the USA. He gave us a big order. In good faith, we started the order. He promised that he would go back and open an L/C. The L/C was opened but in his own father's firm's account. Half the order was with his own father.

Everything was right with the merchandise, but bad luck for us, the whole family was mad. They didn't know what they were doing. The entire shipment was ready, but the labels which were to come from the United

States never arrived till the expiration date of the L/C. Ultimately, they couldn't manage things properly, and the entire shipment was left with us. We were back to square one.

Meanwhile, the Canadian buying agency also went into oblivion. The buyer was working for some retail chain, and he quit. Now again there was no work, and the filth of that jeans shipment was all that I was left with. My wife had a cousin in Bombay.

She called and mentioned that there was somebody she had immense faith in who did auto writing, and he would be coming to Delhi, and we should see him. His name was Ruzbeh N. Bharucha, a Parsi fellow. Anyway, when Ruzbeh came, Preeti and I went to see him. We asked him about the shipment. Point-blank he said that the shipment was not and never going anywhere and that I should stop thinking about it. It was a total loss; that was it. This was pretty blunt, but that was how this guy was. He would communicate with Sai Baba of Shirdi.

He said, 'Baba wants you to go to Gurgaon and get involved in property business'. I always had sort of disliked property agents. The image of a property agent was not comforting at all. I asked him if I could do something else. He replied, 'Who are you to decide?' A couple of days back, my property agent had come to ask for my plot. He had a buyer. He had asked me what I was doing, and somehow it came out of me that I was searching for a profession. He offered me to join him. I had denied him until then. Now I remembered and thought to myself that probably the divine wanted me to do it.

I told Ruzbeh that there was this guy who offered me an opportunity. He said that the guy was like a dark forest but that I would join him. He also said, 'You sell your GKII flat and go to Gurgaon'. I said, 'But there is no need to displace myself. I am already selling my plot, and that would suffice for a lot of my needs.' He replied, 'It will get sold even when you will not be in the house'. Anyway, I said, 'Not everything you have to listen to'. So I didn't make any effort to sell it. I didn't tell any brokers to sell it.

A couple of weeks later, I was playing cricket on a Sunday. My cousin called my wife and said that his friend from Moradabad was in town and looking for a house in GKII, and he suggested our house, so he asked us to show it to her. Preeti agreed and showed the house. This lady liked it and was ready to give advance payment. Preeti tried calling me, but my mobile was in my bag andI was on the ground. Preeti took the advance payment from her. When I came home and came to know about it, I didn't react and accepted the whole thing, remembering Ruzbeh.

I was going to Gurgaon everyday. I joined my agent as a partner. I had located a bigger plot in the vicinity where I had earlier sold one and mentioned it to my brother-in-law in Indore. He said that he was ready to buy 50 percent of it. There were two options available for plot numbers 95 and 96. Preeti's cousin sent a book on Swamiji written by Ruzbeh. I got the book and called

Sarvesh (my brother-in-law in Indore). He was having problems at his factory. I asked him to go to Bangalore and meet Swamiji. I was sceptical that he would ask one million questions, but very promptly he said, 'Okay, let's go. I am in B'bay. You come tomorrow, and from Bombay we shall go together.' I got my one-way ticket on my credit card and took a flight to Bombay. I had the book and the address of the mandir, and the telephone number of Swamiji was mentioned there. I started calling that number and asked for Swamiji. **I realized that as long as you are trying to do things to t**he best of your ability, obviously, using your mind, you still are in the domain of polar opposites, and therefore, we keep lingering between Sukha and Dukha, good and bad, profit and loss.

The level of mind polarity exists; therefore, inevitably the opposite occurs, see all negative emotions and opposite values come out of the mind, peace, joy, love etc is your nature, as a whole, you will have both.

We also mentioned that *'you cannot treat the mind at the level of the mind', meaning once the opposite occurs, what one does* is again try to solve with his mind (obviously). But you will not be absolved of the opposites, which will exist, no matter what, so to go beyond the opposites, you have to allow the bigger mind to take charge of the situation or you **allow the divinity/cosmos** to take the decision. That decision will have no opposite but the higher good only, where opposite doesn't exist. You may call this surrender, which was the root message of Shri Krishna's Geeta, or you can call it being consciousness or witnessing consciousness, which was the root message of Ashtavakra 's Gita.

The mind is a machine, which works on your experiences of the past. This is a sure limitation, a lopsided one. Any lopsided decision cannot give you the best result, the just result. The opposite has to happen. On past experiences, maths can come out. Science can come. Our process can be managed, not life. Life is not the result of the past alone. Life is limitless. Vastness cannot be derived out of limited possibilities. Any decision by anybody, mind driven ever taken, which has given satisfaction.

Even amongst the very greats, in the end, you would find they didn't achieve anything which tested time.

The relationship between the mind and consciousness is time. You take time out of the mind, and the mind drops automatically. When we say be in the present moment, it only implies that you take time out of the equation. You become Being Consciousness. Oscillation between the past and the future in the mind has to be removed. Time has to get out of the picture. Then only you can be in the present. Buddha gave the Sutra: watch your breath. Do it practically. The moment you put attention to your breath, watch it. You would notice the thought stops. Your subconscious stops. The bombardment of thoughts stops. You will experience silence, silence of the subconscious. You will begin to be present.

This should be your practice. Increase your awareness to be with your presence, being conscious. Anything which comes out of your mind is not worth it. Only that which comes out of no mind, the silence, when it comes out, is of consequence, is of higher good, is of worth.

Often people get into this argument of how you can be in business and not use your mind. Nobody is saying do business without your mind. Business, in fact, can be only done with the mind, but an aware mind, not a mind which only wants to maximize profits. Maximizing profits ultimately is a lopsided one-dimensional thinking. Life is not one-dimensional. It will topple awareness and then topple you. When you are doing business, two emotions are prevalent, greed and fear. When you work through greed, then only greed works. In greed, intellect does not function; only greed works.

In greed comes the emotions of anxiety and fear. Your actions can never be right under the influence of these emotions. They will suck you. You will make mistakes, and the result then can only be loss. In business you have two things: transactions and profits. If you focus on profit, the transaction will be in jeopardy. Usually, people focus on profit. The reverse isn't possible. Profits can only be a natural outcome of focusing on the transactions.

If you see this whole economic crisis, which began in the USA, where people swear by what is taught in business schools, it is the last word in economics, the much-talked-about algorithm. But I guess looking at the result and then the crises, world over, because these days every company is global and connected. Every country is facing problems.

This must have been a mind-driven economy that could have given only this result. Maximization of profit based on the theory of the mind can give only this result. The opposite had to take place. Theories based on past experiences and algorithms can be at best suggestive, not definite. Life behaves differently and not on fixed parameters and patterns. Life is not maths, neither is it linear in its approach. The mind only knows complication and in the end destroys. The madness of the mind will take over, the whole theory of leverage, maximizing. You lose awareness. You are doomed because you become linear in your approach, lopsided.

To achieve the goals set by the mind, which are unnatural in nature, this is what I call maximizing, expecting more than you can get.

You have given controls to the mind. The mind is now controlling you and your business. It's deadly. You have forgotten that the mind can only destroy and complicate and create unrests. With such a mind like an idiot, we expect the best of the best result to happen to us. Well, what can I say? Totally insane. This crisis is also totally just the result of an insane mind. Life keeps teaching us lessons in the shape of such crisis, but we never learn to look at the mind and learn not to totally give control to the insane guy in you, which is the mind. The whole practice of becoming aware is to drop the mind, not give it total control.

Regarding that shipment, my brother and I tried it for two years. Not even a *kabari* (rag seller) would buy it. It was given to a *kabari*, who never gave any money. Meanwhile, I was searching for a house in Gurgaon. My date was nearing to give possession of the GK flat to the buyer. After searching for almost three weeks, a junior in the office of that property firm that I joined showed me a ground floor of a five-hundred-yard house, which was never used by anyone. I entered the house, and I could see a lot of green in the backyard. Somehow I liked it. A good feeling came to me. I called Ruzbeh. He asked if it had a thin sort of main gate and if it had a Neem tree at the backyard. I was halfway down from Gurgaon to Delhi. I went back and saw and confirmed to him that both things he mentioned were there. He said, 'Baba is giving you this as gift. Baba spent all his life under the Neem tree, so this is a gift. Go ahead and buy it.' I called my partner. He called the owner, and the deal was fixed.

There was this caretaker who lived in the servant's quarters, since it was never used.

There was a termite issue in Gurgaon. I was renovating it. Once I visited after three weeks, nearing the completion of the interior, I saw that the Neem tree was cut, and there was no tree now. I immediately called Ruzbeh. He was furious. He said, 'I told you this tree was important. Your entire growth depended on this tree. You should have ensured its existence.' I said, 'I will get many more need trees planted'. But he was furious. He said, 'The tree should come out of the same tree. What you do now is ask forgiveness from the tree.

Everyday light a candle and pray and request it to come out.' For six months I prayed to the tree, until one day my wife saw a tiny little shoot come out of it. We were so happy. We talked to Ruzbeh. He said, 'It's good. Now how much ever the tree will grow, you will grow the same.' The whole thing sounded a little strange, but my faith was also becoming airtight. Now in retrospect, if I have to see, then this was so true, unbelievable.

My partner gave me a separate office at the Bristol Hotel, a small cabin space. Every day I would come and sit and think how I would do this business. Where would I get customers and so on? I didn't know anything about Gurgaon and the business, so I asked my partner if we could take an ad in the newspaper to sell the property available with us. The ad came on Sunday. I was playing cricket, and a phone call came in. I fixed the time to meet and show a flat in Heritage City in Gurgaon on M.G.Road.

I reached Gurgaon and started going up and down M.G.Road but couldn't find Heritage City. I called my partner and asked, 'I can't locate Heritage City, and the client is about to arrive'. He said, 'If you don't know where Heritage City is, then God can only help you and put the phone down'. Somehow I arrived and showed the property. They liked it, and the deal was done. I was over the moon.

Sitting long hours in the office alone, I would think which property segments I should do. Because I didn't have muscle power, I thought land should be out. Similarly, farm should be out. I even struck out plots as it would have cash components involved, and all my life being in exports, I had only seen bank transactions. I was also good in paperwork, contracts, and so on; so I zeroed in on flats and offices of the top 5 developers of Gurgaon.

Meanwhile, when Sarvesh and I reached Bangalore, we met Swamiji at the entrance only. He was very receptive and never gave off any feeling that I was meeting him for the first time, although he seemed busy. The Havan of Devi was to take place in an hour. I found out that he would give prediction to everyone after the Havan. The mandir was in a house which was built by him only, and he used to reside on the second floor. Somehow we went to the second floor. I met Ruzbeh also. Swamiji was his guru as well. He told me to go inside his room. It was difficult to go inside. The room was already filled with a lot of people close to Swamiji. Anyway, they were making him wear a saree, and suddenly, he started looking different. His eyes popped. He was getting out of control, as if he was possessed. Yes, infact, Devi had come to him.

He started talking in the old Sanskrit language of India. He started giving blessings. I also took Devi's blessing, but now what I saw was out of this world. His people burnt camphor tablets and put them on the ground. He was walking on them as he started to go down to conclude the *havan*. He was walking on the burnt camphor as if he was walking in the garden, but he was oozing out of his own self. Also, people had burnt camphor tablets in thali for *puja*. He was also eating them like Cadbury gems. This shook me up. I thought to myself, *A human can't put burning camphor on his tongue. It's impossible.* He sat in a small room downstairs where Devi was established and started giving predictions to everyone present there. There was a long queue. We met one Gupta Ji there, and he suggested that we should come tomorrow at noon, and he would give us prediction in private. In any case, today was more or less like a blessing only. We arrived the next day and sat with him. He said, 'I can only give one prediction. You guys decide.' Since Sarvesh had a Public limited company and his problem was much bigger than mine, I told him to give Sarvesh the prediction. I didn't get a prediction, which I wanted so desperately, which of course I got later after a few months, in which he told me to get into property business, although I asked him to look for something else as doing property business after garment exports didn't sound exciting enough.

Regarding the plot which I was buying, I asked Swamiji which number I should buy, B95 or B96. He said, 'Devi wants to gift you B96'. For the meeting with the seller, my partner called the seller's office in Delhi for me.

The meeting began, and the seller told us that his plot was 95 and not 96. My partner looked at me and knew I wouldn't buy 95, and there was some confusion in the communication with the seller, but the seller had asked his secretary to bring the file of the plot. They were an exporters and a big investors. There were many properties. The file came, and he looked at it and said, 'Sorry, it's plot number 96 only'.

I could see the divine work involved in it. I just simply bought at the first price he quoted and took forty-five days to pay and paid him advance payment. I was very happy and informed Sarvesh because he was a 50 percent partner in it. He said, 'OK, no issues'. He would pay, but there was still time to pay, but the date of payment was nearing. I told Swamiji that I had taken the plot and Sarvesh was also a partner in it and would pay 50 percent. He said, 'This is a gift to you from Devi. Sarvesh wouldn't be able to pay. Only you will buy it.' A few days later, I got a call from Sarvesh, and he informed me that he wouldn't be able to contribute. He didn't have funds at the moment.

There were a few launches of flats that came up, and I was very successful in selling them. In one and a half years' time. I met Swamiji again in Bangalore on havan day. In his prediction, he told me to start a property business of my own and leave my partner. 'Devi wants you to it do on your own'. These were his words. But that meant setting up an office, staff, and so on. And more so, the developers didn't know me.

My partner was an established brand. In this business, credibility plays a major role, for which people should know you. You should have a track record and so on.

Also, I thought that the moment I told my partner that I was quitting, he would not give me my commissions. I asked Swamiji the same question, he said, 'Don't worry. This is Devi's problem, not yours. Moreover, this is her money.' I came back to Delhi, picked up the phone, called my partner, and told him I was quitting. He just took off because by now I had become a cash cow for him. His immediate reaction was, 'If you quit, I shall not even pay you even twenty-five paise'. I told him, 'I have not asked for money. I am informing you. That's your discretion to pay or not. My guru has told me to quit.' He was angry and said, 'How can you make such decisions based on some Baba's saying?' Anyway, for me the decision was a leap of faith. It was like jumping off a cliff. Without using my mind, I jumped. I didn't involve myself. I didn't allow my mind to intervene, because I knew my mind would never allow me. Also, I was to receive such amounts after a long time in life. I had not seen any sizeable money for far too long, and this was my hard work for one and a half years. Anyway, I quit and started on my own. If I was to look back, this was such a good decision. My partner gave me payments later barring a deduction of forty percent.

I then would take blessings from him, before doing a project, so that it's beneficial not only for me but more so for my clients.

My main concern would be my clients. If they made money, it became my kick. Once my business associate asked me to do a project on an exclusive basis, which is called underwriting in our real estate terms. I told him yes. I asked Swamiji, and he told me not to do so. The developer was not trustworthy. I told my friend I would not be doing it without specifying any reasons. He found it really funny because (a) I had said yes the previous day and (b) we could have made a lot of money in a few weeks. Later, I learnt that the developer had landed in jail. Besides my due diligence, his nod was very important. It was the divine nod. Money never mattered to me, in front of his call.

Two years later, after buying plot number 96, I sold it for four times the price that I had bought it. I was getting two plots of 350 square yards together in the same colony. I asked Swamiji about it, and he told me to buy it with my eyes closed. This was now even a bigger gift. I was going to Pakistan to watch a cricket series between India and Pakistan in 2006. I was on a train to the Wagah border, and my office colleague from my previous partner's office called. They were his client's plots. I couldn't hear much, especially the price part, but I told him to take the advance payment from Preeti at home, and the rest we would settle once I came back. Obviously, the price I bought them for was higher because I didn't negotiate one bit. He was also surprised. I still have them. I asked Swamiji later whether I should build anything. He told me, 'You should have started building on it yesterday. It will help you.' It took me two years to build. Now, since six years, that property is on rent. Now, since markets are down for the past three years, that property is taking care of my monthly expenditures.

I was growing each day, in business, as was my *Neem tree*, or you can say as the tree was growing, I was growing as well, although Swamiji, during his first prediction, had told me that by 2010, I would be financially and professionally very strong; but to comprehend that at that time was not possible for me. I was more bothered about money for my return trip from Bangalore to Delhi.

Things were becoming better and better professionally. I was climbing the ladder very fast. I was becoming a prominent and reliable figure in this industry. My lifestyle took a dynamic change; and suddenly, swanky cars, Prada, and Gucci were becoming a day-to-day wear for me. I fully surrendered to the idea that if you give your 100 percent, what comes naturally to you is what is good for you. Rather that, what looks more profitable. Give the client the right advice and don't even expect that they would buy, rather than manipulate them for your profits. I will give my 100 percent to the best of my ability; the rest I would leave to Devi's will.

Deep down, one had the understanding that one is taken care of by the divine, so a lot of acceptance of what is was there.

On a larger deal, I would tell my mind before entering the meeting, 'Please, boss, let me do it. You don't come in between. **You relax. And if you are operating from the intellect and not the complications or subjectivities of the mind, you operate better. Then you are not manipulating the deal.'**

I joined a consortium called G9. We are a group of six brokerage firms. The group was formed to collectively represent and deal in bulk to negotiate a better deal with the developers. For clients, when the markets were booming came the theory of underwriting the goods with the developers, which means you commit to sell a large quantity by paying a 5 to 10 percent deposit with the developers, and you get the goods at a cheaper value and sell at a higher value and make that extra buck.

When I looked at this phenomenon, I thought to myself, *This is a greed game, and my business is to get the best deal for my client.* Brokerage can only be the natural outcome of selling, by concentrating on brokerage and not the product or the developer or the interest of my investor and whether the product will perform or not, investors' interest is diluted a great deal.

Since I am the oldest member of the team, and everybody listens to me, I turned the whole underwriting game upside down. We would represent as a consortium to sell large quantities but not give any deposit, but would negotiate with the developer and get the best deal for the investors, which would bring value to the developers and the investor at the same time.

Initially, it was difficult to get goods without deposit, but later it became an accepted fact with developers that G9 would not give deposit.

We were well accepted in the market, and if you check, shifting focus from extra bucks, we were able to sell more flats and earn maybe more than making in between margin and picking up some rubbish developers' goods and putting my investors' interest in jeopardy.

The idea is not to allow your mind to always look at things through greed. If you are in business, it will seldom work or never work.

When the bigger mind works for you, or the cosmos works for you, or the divine works for you, you will get what is required before you require it.

I met Ruzbeh, and he said that I should now have some rental income. After fifteen days, I got a call from a broker that someone wanted my guesthouse on a long term lease, and the same was put on rent immediately the next week. Another example, markets were bad for two years. Nothing was getting sold. There was no liquidity. I needed one of my properties to get sold to get liquidity and get my loan EMI reduced. It was becoming imperative. Out of the blue, one day one of my properties got sold.

Your problem got resolved without your effort only because you are not there in between you and the divine. Then the divine will take care of you beautifully. You will be given before you need it.

After 2013, the markets were in a real bad shape. Not much was happening in real estate. I needed another venture to start.

To my surprise, I don't know from where this French company came, and I got the all-India rights to sell their products. We had to import these products from France. There came the suggestion that the import duty was around 34 percent, and if we under invoiced, we could make a lot of money. 'This is how most people do their imports. It's normal. It's business requirement,' I told them, that the business was given to me by the divine to do it correctly, and it should run. Why the hell on earth should I manipulate the business given to me to maximize gains? Just comply with the rules, keep it simple, and it will run successfully.

Manipulating the business is not my business.

This is what I mean by the mind complicating things. One should be aware of this. The moment you come in the picture, you start complications. In all this, what was common was that *I wasn't manipulating any result or anything. I am simply getting it before I require it. There are many such examples I can give. The point is, simply get out of your own way and allow the cosmos to work for you. It will never fail you. For sure you will get all that you require.* See, you exist at the core. The mind is at the periphery. Anything coming out of the mind is a function at the periphery. Often people misunderstand and mix the two and remain in unrest and unease. First, be established in your core. You should take the decision through the core, devoid of the mind, but give 100 percent with intellect/mind at the periphery. A decision taken from the core will not carry fear, greed, anxiety, and so on. It will be in most cases the right decision.

Then do what is required to be done at the periphery. Give your 100 percent effort, but usually, we do the reverse. We take a decision from the mind, and later, when we don't get the desired result, we look at the core, or you may say look at God. *Please save me. Take care of me.* But the reverse is not possible.

With the mind, humans have no doubt achieved a lot of progress in providing luxury and comfort to themselves. There are many achievements in the field of science. No doubt if the West pursued the progress they did achieve, they have achieved a lot more than the East, who only depended on religion or spirituality; and as a result, they are poor and left behind a lot by the west. But the point remains that both didn't achieve a balanced growth. We need balance. Only one is dangerous, lopsided, and therefore, not full in result. The West has already started looking at the East for spirituality, and the East has started with progress in the material world. We need to balance both to be able to get peace with progress.

You ask a guy who has achieved a lot in terms of material, 'Do you possess peace?' The answer would be no, and in reverse the answer is also no. In the material world, be aware of your inner mechanism. Then you could say, 'You have done well'. If you have done well in the material world and are one with yourself, no stresses, anxiety, fear, jealousy, and other negative emotions, then you have done well. Otherwise, it's lopsided.

See, all these emotions are on the outside of you, and business is also an activity of the outside. Complete stillness, peace, fearlessness, compassion, contentment, and so on come from within.

Remember we talked that every chakra has the opposite values exists.

If you go too much outside of yourself, which is the world, although in your mind you call it the material world, you will definitely experience everything else but inner quality of peace, love compassion, satisfaction, contentment, and so on. It's obvious, so we need balance. How balance can be created was a question that I lived with for over five years. The little that I have understood, I will share with you.

To start with, I would say material is not at all bad. Creating comfort is not bad. It cannot be. In hunger you will only think of the body. Think about yourself, survival. You would still be in the mind and body, thought and emotion. The question was to go beyond. Comfort will, in fact, make things easier to achieve. Material abundance will also give you the experience of it, and then it is easier to drop your obsession with it. Come out of it and start looking at it objectively. If you were to live in the material world, say, a business or job, remember that the mind can never be dropped. The mind will exist, but now, it's under your command. It's not interfering with you. You are not getting sucked. You are not acting based on emotions or obsessions. The intensity is much reduced. The time taken to come out has reduced drastically; therefore, you are not acting out of emotion. Remember, we are talking of the chattering mind, subconscious mind, or as I have been calling here, a mind which loves complications, not intellect. Rather, your intellectual skills are more sharpened.

You are getting the correct answer without effort. **If it's under your command, consider that it has dropped.** An intellect or logical mind devoid of the chattering mind can take a decision based on merit, even if that means a longer route or time or effort, but it will be a correct one.

Don't be in a hurry to achieve anything. Let the dropping take place on its own. Any effort in this direction will result in manipulation of the mind. Then you are treating it at the level of the mind. Changing any arrangement will not help. Start witnessing. You would then find that you are delinked with your thought processes and start looking at it. It will start to loosen its grip on you.

No longer are you caught up in it. It is not driving you anymore. It becomes futile. The bombardment of thoughts stops. You start feeling that you are free of them. It will also help you attach and detach quickly. You could then move from material to spiritual, periphery to core, with a lot of ease. Remember, you can not avoid the worldly world, so give your 100 percent while you are there and if you are in the inner world then also give your 100 percent and don't be in the worldly world at the same time. Always remember the tightrope walker. Then no situations can create unwanted stress.

You don't become your thought and be in it for a long time, so it can't have any negative impact on you. Remember to keep working at them only. Give time. Don't rush. Make it a practice. It will not happen in a jiffy. Let it take time, no hurry. That's the practice sages have also talked about.

'You shouldn't die before you know yourself.'

Once you start to know yourself, you will create a beautiful balance between the core and the periphery or (AATMA) consciousness and mind. The need to look at the mind is in a way to look at Aatma. You don't know anything about Aatma - the Deathless. You can also not know beyond the fact that you have heard and read in Vedas that it exists within you. That's all you know about it. What is the use of it if you don't even know that it exists? But by cessation of the mind, you might get a glimpse of it, or you can say you will come to know that something else also exists, or you aren't your mind.

Then the periphery will start to crumble and you start to function through the core. Your periphery is made up of all your diseases, mind emotions, Vaasnas, Indriyas, madness of the mind, life situations, differences, religions, and so on.

Why life situations give stress or sadness or restlessness, it's only that the mind perceives the situation like that and gives you a sense that things have not fallen in place per your expectations; therefore, they are not right. Actually, your perceptions are based on or come out of your conditioned mind. You have to realize this fact. This mind can only behave on a logical axis, along with emotional conditioning, and therefore can never give you the right result, because the right result will end or kill the mind. So how can it allow? It can only give you a solution, which will tell you to go further into madness, a bigger desire from before, a bigger dream to chase.

Remember, desire can only multiply. There is no other purpose of it. Your sense organs become more rigid when you live through them, and then they have to have a bigger experience each time than before, but you can't come out of it, unless they are looked at.

The right result can only be to give you peace. That's where you started to do a thing, to give you satisfaction.

When you are at peace, the mind doesn't exist. The mind will never give you the right result, so therefore, a balance is required in this world to exist. I am not telling you to stop using your intellectual mind. It is essential to have it. You can't exist otherwise, but living through the mind is dangerous, of no use. It's madness, nothing else. Balance is the answer.

Actually, if you want to know what spirituality is without any speculations about God and Aatma, see it beyond the physical and logical mind. Spirituality only begins once you have seen the futility of the physical and logical. Then only you go beyond the karma bracket. The karma domain exists only when you are in the physical and logical mind.

More consciousness means more awareness, and any decision taken in awareness will always result in good and good alone.

It will be for your growth, but with the mind. Then you make a decision based on the state of the mind then, which is full of emotional fear, greed, and so on. How can it be totally good for you? The moment mind is there. You are not conscious.

Then the decision is also not total, not worthy. The mind can only make strategies of self-defeat. A lopsided decision is the outcome. The law is simple. The more presence you have, the more correct you are, the more total you are. Otherwise, economic crashes happen andshall happen, as well as other disasters. If you are in the mind, then your breathing is not normal and harmonized, which means that you have a distorted breathing pattern, which means that it's coming out of some negative emotion. Then a decision based on that negative emotion will carry the negative result. How much intellectually do you try and achieve the desired result?

People in business often talk about desire as a goal. See, in desire, you are feverish about reaching the goal you set. There is no problem with the goal, but to act through your desire to reach your goal creates a problem. You start to manipulate the business, and then the same desire will manipulate you. You are in a state of unawareness. Now you are sucked by desire. You can go on wasting life. Desire will keep changing and keep becoming bigger. You are now getting spent by desire. You set a goal, no issue, but don't be desirous of the result. It works like this: A thought will bring a corresponding emotion. The emotion will suck you and give you thoughtfulness. Thought then takes over your being with the ego, fear, greed, and so on at the helm of it. How on earth can it give you the right result? For sure it will give you lopsided results.

In business, you go out worldly, and then you are entangled in the polarities of good and bad, success and defeat, winning and losing.

Your whole life is then spent on that domain. Then you haven't seen life. You haven't lived a life. You have just spent it in futility.

When you go inside and know yourself, you then know that a single axis can't give you satisfaction. If you only spend on futile things and efforts, going inside may not get you the most possible profits, but surely a balance of both can give joy, abundance, and peace. It's knowing of the futility of the material world. Our 'worldly' world and knowing the inside world of peace and satisfaction can give you the right balance of the right way of living, peaceful, joyous living the abundant way. *You are then rocking.*

The mind works on logic. A logical graph is linear, but a life graph is not linear. It could be anything but linear. This is where the problem lies. In business, I say a logical mind cannot get the best result. If the logical mind could achieve the best result, then it would be very easy for anyone to be successful. Everybody would be a millionaire. Also, with a mind to act out of your impressions of the past, or the prevailing emotions, or just to chase success blindly, then obviously, you are to manipulate a lot of things, including yourself. See, when you try to achieve something, that means you have decided to achieve it. That means you are not open to any other possibilities which life throws at you. This thinking is a single axis. That is one-directional. Then you would try to manipulate everything and yourself.

You can never be successful. For success to come, your act should be devoid of the mind and manipulation, devoid of emotion.

Even if, for instance, you get success, then you also carry a certain emotion which will have negativity.

Success is not achieved. You will strive for bigger achievements. The desire will then take over. It's never-ending then. You are engulfed in desire. Desire can only multiply.

You will get spent on it your whole life. You know, one has to keep monitoring what it is that he is getting spent on, remember the joy isn't in the subject, for example, if two people are on a lake with beautiful scenery all around, one person is saying how beautiful and the other is saying how boring. The same thing is perceived differently by two different individuals. Joy lies in the chewing of it in your mind and getting spent Once you are aware of this fact, this helps you not to get driven by the mind.

In fact, if you increase your level of awareness, and you can keep looking at yourself getting spent on, you have started to come out of the clutches of your mind. Then you are not chasing anything with a preset emotion or manipulating anything. Then you are just doing your job, without expectations, without manipulations.

This act will get you the best result, even if the result may look a little less, but you will be satisfied totally, not hankering, not feeling any lack. That's what I call a good result. Less is most of the time more, and more is seldom more. In business, it will always be less because you are riding a horse of desire now. I have seen and met a lot of businessmen. I saw one thing was common: they were all running men, men of the future. You can't have a dialogue with a running man.

You can't discuss anything because he is not present. In fact, greed and fear are very evident emotions emitting out of them.

In the theory of less is more, less or more is also of the mind. It's relative. If you see, I advocate it very strongly, not because I am a pessimist or do not want to achievesomething, but purely on the grounds that I am OK with whatever result has come out of the act. I am satisfied with any result. In the same manner, even if it was less or more, then in my next act, I can again give 100 percent without being anxious about achievement.

A good result is a consequence of a good act. An act done in its purity, devoid of greed, fear, or any other emotion, is a good act; and the result can be satisfying. Where is the question of less or more? It doesn't arise, and that's a good result. This may seem very contradictory in this material world, where success is rated high, and you have to compete in whatever you do. You have to be number one. You have to maximize your profits.

I will give you a very interesting example of a builder in NCR, when he started out, let's say, he had 150 acres of prime land and an FD of 1,000 crores. After five years, rigorously striving to be on top, maximizing profits, and taking all top consultants, in a rising market in NCR, he is now finished with his prime land and staring at a debt of over 1,500 crores. Obviously, I am sure he is getting spent on his mind every second of the day. In further complications, he can't have peace.

The quality of his breathing pattern will be full of anxiety, fear, and greed; he has moved away from a harmonized axis. Now, he is acting out of emotions and manipulations.

For me, he is finished, not business-wise. He may possess millions, but it's not worth it. This is a vicious cycle people get into. Now, do you call it a success? Yes, people do in society, but I call it a failure and a total madness. The mind killed him in his own mind. He is a dead man walking. He cannot have peace. His breathing cannot get back to its axis of harmony. He got sucked by himself. No doubt, he now has three hundred acres of land, but not prime, not sellable. He will now be furnishing debt and working to pay debt. He has become a labourer working to pay debt. I can see the unrest. I am sure he will not be delivering a good product.

He has no money to finish existing projects. Obviously, he will cut corners, and the product will suffer. On the contrary, if and only if he had not acted out of greed, and finished existing projects properly, he would have had probably 3,000 crores because markets were booming in this period. It wold be a cash-rich company, and people would have queued up for JV with their land. Now tell me, less is more or not, and above all, rich is a state of the mind, which would have taken him to new heights. This is the result when markets boom, and the mind can seriously drive you mad, totally unaware, insane. Actually, you don't need a reason to be happy, but surely you require a reason to be unhappy, and this can be used as a big help in recognizing that you are working in the mind domain if you are unhappy.

Please note that and use it to your advantage. This will remind you that you are in the mind domain. Then it's easy to come out of mere looking at that reason in a way that it will drop and find yourself back on the axis. You have to forget the right and wrong argument at this point. You have to remember that right or wrong is coming out of your mind. It's relative. There is nothing completely right or completely wrong. Right and wrong are very much a mind game.

The reason is polarity, because of the mind, but the actual phenomenon is remembering to see that you are in the mind zone, and then the whole thing drops automatically. This will go a long way in coming out of the mind. See, at the core, you have consciousness, where right and wrong don't exist; but at the periphery, which is the mind, right and wrong, profit and loss, happiness and sadness and so on, polarity exists.

In the mind, polarity exists, or the opposite exists, and therefore, whatever the mind proves today will disprove it tomorrow. That's why with any arrangement of the mind to set today, the mind will lose interest after some time and want to change because the other pole is pulling. That's why dissatisfaction is experienced because at one pole you can't remain for a long time. It has to go to the other pole. People talk about renouncing the world. Go to the Himalayas or jungles and undertake spirituality in ashrams, where they can be away from the world. For sure, they can't achieve it.

They are now wanting to move to the other pole, from the world to no world. They are mistaken. If you see, there is a polarity shift happening, nothing else. From one arrangement of the world, you are going to another arrangement, or pole, so to say, a no world, from rest to activity, from activity to rest. That's all. That's why in life also, you have night and day, night for rest and day for activity. If I can explain it in a simple way, I will give you another example.

There was this prostitute who lived outside a monastery, and a monk lived in the monastery. The prostitute was not allowed to enter the monastery. All her life, she kept thinking, *If, and only if, I can enter the monastery and meditate, I will become so happy.* On the other hand, the monk would think, *If, and only if, I could sleep with this prostitute, I will be happy.*

Both were on one pole and dying to go to the other pole. The opposite attracts. The opposite exists on the mind level. You can spend your whole life in this polarity game, without realizing it; therefore, I say one has to be aware and see this phenomenon. It's nothing but shift in polarity. Normally, we see most of us start to get into spirituality or religious acts at the age fifty-two and above. Doing this is good, and I am not saying, 'Why do you do it?' But look at the phenomenon. The mind has become tired. The body has also become tired. It's from activity to rest, the polarity shift.

Don't think that doing this will now make you totally happy. You have to go beyond the polarity or the mind to be really happy. At least awareness about this phenomenon will get you to see it objectively and then come out of it. So life is a balancing act, from periphery to core and core to periphery.

The time taken to come out of one and go to the other is what your growth is, and that is your practice. You can't leave the world and be in the world. You can't be at the core, so work like a tightrope walker. Keep balancing. You will have some great results in life.

Some meditation is required daily. All Gurus are teaching meditation, and it's the biggest thing happening these days. If you watch carefully in this ten to fifteen minute meditation, what is happening is that the mind is going from chattering to the other pole of non chattering, activity to rest. Obviously, if you experience it, you say you are relaxed. Now, this is good, if it happens; but the real thing is that, once you have recognized that the mind exists, and you are a slave to it, then to use it in the manner and fashion that you want. You need to go beyond it. This temporary polarity shift in meditation is going to help a little initially but will not make you a ruler of your mind, unless you understand that the mind is using you, and you are being spent by its whim and fancy. But once you have recognized it, then it starts to loosen its grip gradually, and then even looking at it will help you come out of it and go beyond. I think there are two very strong ways: breath and silence.

That's why, I say, 'Be in the world totally and also leave it totally'. Your time taken to come back to the world and the world to consciousness should keep lessening.

Remember, if you are in one pole, you are in the mind domain.

To sum up, the first thing is to recognize the mind and driven by it all the time and now to come out of its clutches. One can approach this in two ways: The first approach is to be on the harmonized axis of your breath that will take care of the emotional indulgences and thought bombardment. Once this is slowed down and starts to go southwards, you will find a lot of peace setting in. Contentment will come. Naturally, you start to live in happiness and experience joy in life and in whatever you are doing. You will be satisfied. That means you will be on zero value. Contentment is being on zero value. Then the mind is not controlling you, or the mind is not troubling you, or you are not sucked by it, which means you are not getting spent by it. That's a great achievement anyway. Once the mind doesn't control you, then it's easy to align yourself with the SELF.

Also, you start to connect with the cosmic energy field. Then everything can be put on neutral. As they say for cars, 'put it in neutral'. Neutral means no energy is required to propel the car. It runs on its own. Here, the bigger mind or Divinity will take control of your things, and naturally as when you require anything, you would find that happens for you. But again let me remind you, don't orchestrate anything. That will be manipulation. Again you come in the ambit of the mind.

The second approach can be observing silence. Remember, at the helm of every emotion, there is silence. So observing silence of the chattering mind will also help the mind subside and gradually lose control on you. Also, the chattering of the mind will stop.

The more the breakages exist by observing the silence you create in the continuity of chattering by the subconscious, the more you gain control of your chattering mind, the more awareness will come of the chattering mind. Then the breakages created by the chattering of the mind gradually drop. You will be more present, and the more you are present, the less and less you are sucked by it. Remember, the mind will not die. It will exist. And if you treat it with the mind, it's nothing but manipulation of it. If it persists, silence is the answer for it to naturally drop or loosen its grip.

Actually, breath and silence are interconnected. If you observe your breath, then you notice that the chattering mind has no thought and vice versa. Observing silence to achieve a harmonized breathing is difficult, but the practice should be observing the breath, inhaling from the navel, and going upwards. You would immediately notice no thought and silence. It's very simple, and should be in continuous practice, especially when one is bombarded with many thoughts.

I am advocating going in the reverse as a very important phenomenon. If you are in the world, or mind, then you must go in the reverse, rest and activity. The balance of the world and spirituality is very important then. Otherwise, we have innumerable examples of even Gurus going to jail for sex and rape. This will happen if you are on a single axis. You should be moving from the world to the inner world and vice versa with ease.

At the level of the mind, opposites exist. We have looked at this aspect a lot in this book, so I shall say one has to be aware of looking at this phenomenon of the level of the mind or the mind domain. It helps a great deal in not getting stuck in the mind, and therefore, not giving control to the mind as your boss. The more grip of the mind is loosened, the more you will allow Divinity to work for you, the more you will get aligned to the cosmic rhythm, the more you can put your car in neutral. You are then completely taken care of. What you require will come to you before you require it.

With this awareness, you will find everything falling in its place. Everything then drops automatically. There is no effort required. It becomes the natural outcome. The dropping has to be a natural outcome, not any effort. There is no scope of effort in my understanding. I feel that effort is a manipulation of the mind. It can't give any result except the opposite.

Then you are on the path of success, abundance and freedom. Then you are taken care of by the divine or the cosmic energy.

Also, you are free from your own self, and that for me is the biggest detachment. When you can detach yourself from your own self, you are free. This has been my success story, and this is my practice too.

I am not a Guru and I am not preaching anything.

This is only my understanding of life. I am not a good storyteller or writer.

In fact, writing is not my craft. I have deliberately kept the book short and objective in terms of understanding. I think people feel they have not got answers after practicing spirituality, except becoming a part of a cult. You can find answers here because a lot of subjective spirituality is floated around by so-called Gurus. They also keep spirituality on the imaginary axis. There is no clarity. One remains confused and keeps chasing Gurus.

The main purpose of writing this book is it all started with Swami Parthasarathy's words:'That mind is like a child and you've got to control it'. I realized that it means that I am two, not one, and the other has to be controlled. Or if the other is a child or a monkey, and he is controlling me, then it's going to be disastrous. But then I realized that if the only way to control it is by manipulating it and it can't be controlled, then what should I do? How can it naturally be controlled or dropped or at least its intensity lessened? I have been writing this book for more than two decades. I wanted the book to come out of me, rather than writing it. I based it on my personal experiences, I believed this is the only correct way and has helped me on every occasion.

One can exist in this world of extreme competition and adversities with a lot of clarity and poise, instead of getting lost and spent by one's own mind, if one balances like a tightrope walker.

Printed in the United States
By Bookmasters